Rental Property Investing

How to Become an Effective Rental Property Investor

(Develop the Skills to Confidently Analyze and Invest in Multifamily Real Estate)

Derrick Guan

Published By **Bengion Cosalas**

Derrick Guan

All Rights Reserved

Rental Property Investing: How to Become an Effective Rental Property Investor (Develop the Skills to Confidently Analyze and Invest in Multifamily Real Estate)

ISBN   978-1-7750277-6-8

No part of this guidebook shall be reproduced in any form without permission in writing from the publisher except in the case of brief quotations embodied in critical articles or reviews.

Legal & Disclaimer

The information contained in this book is not designed to replace or take the place of any form of medicine or professional medical advice. The information in this book has been provided for educational & entertainment purposes only.

The information contained in this book has been compiled from sources deemed reliable, and it is accurate to the best of the Author's knowledge; however, the Author cannot guarantee its accuracy and validity and cannot be held liable for any errors or omissions. Changes are periodically made to this book. You must consult your doctor or get professional medical advice before using any of the suggested remedies, techniques, or information in this book.

Upon using the information contained in this book, you agree to hold harmless the Author from and against any damages, costs, and expenses, including any legal fees potentially resulting from the application of any of the information provided by this guide. This disclaimer applies to any damages or injury caused by the use and application, whether directly or indirectly, of any advice or information presented, whether for breach of contract, tort, negligence, personal injury, criminal intent, or under any other cause of action.

You agree to accept all risks of using the information presented inside this book. You need to consult a professional medical practitioner in order to ensure you are both able and healthy enough to participate in this program.

Table Of Contents

Chapter 1: Preambles

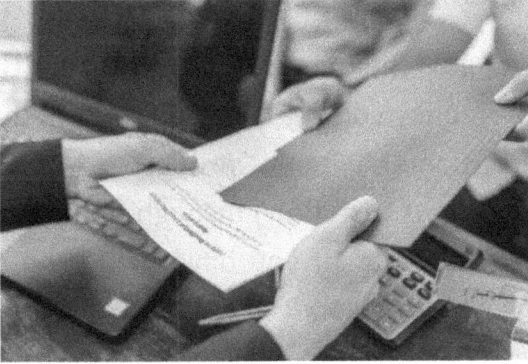

Hello there, you are the next real business billionaires!

Be prepared, because I've got a game-changing chance to offer you the chance to invest in rental properties across the great ole United States! It's an investment opportunity that's sure make you swoon And I'm here today to share all the exciting specifics.

Imagine this scenario that you're seeking an opportunity to earn some money without working in a 9-to-5 work. What do you think?

rental properties are where the action is at! They offer a wealth of advantages that will have your bank account smiling and all your acquaintances asking your personal secret.

We've got the passive income. Yes, that's right - money coming in as you relax and take in the moment. Rental properties can bring this delicious cash flow, through monthly rent payments. It's as if you have your own ATM which doesn't run out of cash.

We must not forget appreciation, dear friend. Real estate is a perverse technique of climbing up the value ladder with the course of time. This means that when you're ready to take cash and sell your property, you might see some huge capital gain. Cha-ching!

Did I talk about the tax benefits? You're ready for an enthusiastic dance in the tax time. Renting properties can open an abundance of benefits and deductions. Consider the tax on your property, mortgage rates repair and maintenance costs--the list is endless. The tax bill you pay just got much more hospitable.

However, here's the true kicker that is equity building. Each mortgage payment that made, you're accumulating equity. This is like stacking those dollars each brick at a time. As time passes this property may rise in value and give you the ability to build wealth.

Well, I can tell that you're thinking, this sounds like it's too good to be true you think? So, prepare yourself to be amazed by another round of it. Rental properties can be a great way to diversify your portfolio of investments. This means that you're not placing all your eggs into one basket. Therefore, even if the stocks market rollercoasters begin creating anxiety Your real estate investments are sure to keep you moving smoothly.

The real ingredient: rentals are a great protection against rising prices. When prices increase the rental income as well as the value of property tends to increase in tandem. This means that your earnings keep in line with the growing cost of living. This means you are always one step ahead.

There's more! This is leverage here, baby. The investment in real estate allows you to borrow money from mortgages to purchase homes for less than the cash needed upfront. This means that you are able to dive into the realm of real estate using less money and use the rental earnings to pay the mortgage costs. Genius, right?

My friend you're now ready to dream big, think large, and put your money into investing. The rental properties you own are the key towards financial security and the life that you've always envisioned. In the United States is your playground and is full of opportunities as well as untapped possibilities.

You're ready to grab your life's challenges head-on, dive into the realm of real estate investing and see your savings increase while sipping pina coladas at the beach.

Are you ready to plunge into the water? Buckle up, my future real estate tycoon. It's going to be a hell of an adventure!

Are you searching to find that perfect rental home that can leave you feeling in the first moment you walk through the front door? You're in luck! you've found the right resource to guide you along the way!

The search for the ideal rental property is a challenging task that is filled with twists and turn, and certainly a portion of ambiguity. Don't fret! I'm here for you to be your trusted companion and rental guru as well as your primary source for all you have to learn about getting that ideal home within America. United States.

It's true that renting isn't about just taking a note and receiving keys. It's about finding that perfect place that fits your needs as if it were a perfect fit and brings smiles every time you step out of the house. We're here to help make sure that you have found precisely that.

In this guide, we'll dive into the enthralling world of renting. The book will explore the latest developments, decode the legal terminology (trust me when I say it's not so scary as you think) as well as equip you with the necessary knowledge and confidence needed to find the home that will leave you feeling as if you've struck the jackpot.

Then we'll get into the details of the process for applying -- what you can expect, and the best way to put your chance, and perhaps there's a secret recipe that will give you an advantage. Lease agreements? Yes, we'll address those as well. Don't get confused by the sea of fine prints.

It's also not all about details. It's also about making your rental home truly appear like your own home. We'll offer some suggestions to keep the property looking great and dealing with landlords in a professional manner and becoming the most cool neighbor in the neighborhood.

Through this journey you'll have me as your guide to point to amazing resources, web-based tools as well as tips and tricks to help you navigate the landscape of renting as a pro. The knowledge and the tools to make informed decisions and start this new part of your journey in a blaze of enthusiasm.

Now, get ready and get your friends on board! We'll open the door to the dream property you've always wanted in which you'll be able to take off your shoes and relax with your feet and unwind in the space you're proud to be able to call your own.

Welcoming you to the wild and beautiful world of rental homes. Let's find that perfect property!

Cheers,

I'm Evelyn

Your Rental Friend and Councilor

BENEFITS AND PROFITABILITY MARGIN OF INVESTING ON RENTAL PROPERTIES IN THE UNITED STATE

Renting properties for rental within the United States offers several benefits and is a lucrative venture.

Discover the many advantages and profits rents that are that are associated with renting property investment:

Passive income from rental properties: Rental properties can provide an ongoing stream of passive income from rent payments every month, which allows you to make cash while not actively working.

Property appreciation Properties in real estate can increase in value over time, thereby raising their value. The appreciation could result in permanent capital gains should you decide to dispose of the home in the near future.

Tax Benefits: Rent property owners have the opportunity to benefit from different tax advantages and deductions including tax on property and mortgage interest, repair and maintenance costs Depreciation, repairs and maintenance, among others. The deductions you receive can lower your tax bill overall.

Equity Building: When you make payments towards the mortgage of the rental property you build equity. In time, the house's worth can rise which can lead to more capital and wealth accumulation.

The diversification of your portfolio: Estate investments offer diversification in your portfolio of investments. They are able to be different than other asset classes, such as bonds or stocks, and could help you balance your investment risk.

Renting property can be used as a hedge against rising inflation. If inflation is rising rent incomes and home values will increase allowing you to stay in the loop or even increase your earnings.

The ability to control investment: In contrast to the other options for investment renting properties provide you with the possibility of having control. You can pick the property, control it, enhance it and establish rental costs for maximum profit.

Short-Term Rental Opportunity: With the growth of websites like Airbnb and Airbnb, short-term rental rentals are now a common alternative for owners of properties. It can result in greater rental earnings, specifically in areas that are desirable as well as during the peak tourist season.

Leverage: Investments in real estate typically require leverage via mortgage financing. You can buy an investment property for a minimal upfront cost, and use the rent to fund the mortgage payment.

Wealth Creation and Retirement Planning Renting property can be used as an investment strategy for building wealth over the long term and aid your retirement plan. Rent-based income from properties may help you build the retirement savings you have and offer an assurance of financial security.

In the years of experience I have gained I have learned that it's crucial to keep in mind that rents the results can differ based on aspects like area, property type rent demand, costs as well as management efficiency. Doing thorough research, doing thorough due diligence and collaborating with professionals in the field of real estate can assist you in maximizing the value and profits of your planned and planned rental property investment portfolio.

STEP BY STEP GUIDE TO INVESTING IN RENTAL PROPERTIES IN THE UNITED STATES

Understanding the Rental Market Trends:

Here are some examples recent developments of the economy of rental properties within the United States, take note of the following:

Rental Demand: The demand for rental is consistently high over the last few years because of numerous factors like changing demographics, challenges to affordability on the housing market and the lifestyle choices. Generations that are younger, like Generation Y and Generation Z, have shown that they prefer renting over than home ownership.

Rent Prices: The cost of renting tend to be increasing across several cities in the United States. But, the pace increases can be wildly according to area. Things like jobs, population growth and the local housing stock as well as demand-driven dynamics affect rent prices.

In the past, low rates of vacancy have been noticed in many important cities. This has led to an increase in renters' competition and the possibility of higher rent for owners of property. It is important to look into specific locations because vacancy rates may be quite different between the cities and communities.

Urbanization as opposed to. Suburbanization COVID-19 caused to shifts in the rental market dynamic. In some urban areas, there was some temporary decreases in demand for rental units and a rise in gap in vacancies, as remote jobs and lifestyle adjustments pushed tenants to look for larger homes in rural or suburban areas. The long-term implications remain unclear, but urban areas could be regaining their popularity as the market changes.

Short-term rentals: Websites such as Airbnb and VRBO have seen a surge in popularity over recent times, offering the opportunity to property owners let their homes in a short-term manner. It is important to be aware of local regulations and market saturation as certain cities have placed limits on rental properties for short-term use.

Legal Considerations:

If you are a property owner who is renting within the United States, there are certain legal aspects you must be aware of prior investing. You should consult a licensed real estate lawyer or attorney that specializes in the field of real estate law, to be sure that you're in compliance with local federal, and state regulations.

Here are a few important legal issues to keep in your mind:

Tenant-Landlord Laws: Get familiar with the landlord-tenant law for the particular state and locality where you are planning to put your money. These laws define the rights and obligations for both tenants and landlords including the lease agreement, security deposit, the increase in rent, eviction processes along with property maintenance. the rights of tenants to privacy.

Fair Housing Laws: Federal fair housing laws ban discrimination on the basis of aspects like race and color, national origin or religion, sexual orientation or familial standing, as well as the presence of disability. Local and state governments may include additional protected categories. It is essential to know and adhere to these laws in advertising and screening tenants, establishing the rental requirements, or managing the property.

Permits and licensing: Certain cities or states will require landlords to have certain licenses or permits in order to manage rentals. The requirements for these can differ which is why it's important to investigate and follow the licensing and permit requirements relevant to your location of investment.

Property Security and Building Codes Check that the property you rent is in compliance with all applicable standards for building codes and safety. Be familiar with the local rules regarding safety in the event of fire, electrical systems plumbing and the structural strength. It is possible to conduct regular inspections in order to ensure conformity.

Zoning as well as Land Use Regulations: Verify that the property you are considering purchasing is zoning for rental use and is in compliance with Zoning regulations in your area.

Tax Obligations: Be aware of the tax consequences associated with rental properties, which includes the federal, state and local taxes. Speak with a tax advisor to ensure that you're in compliance with the filing requirements as well as to comprehend the potential benefits and deductions related to property and rental expenditures.

Insurance Coverage: Proper insurance coverage is crucial for property owners who own rental properties. It is also recommended to speak with an insurance broker to establish the right amount and type of insurance protection for the specific property. This includes the liability insurance and property insurance as well as earthquake or flood insurance based on where the property is located.

Eviction Procedures: Be familiar with the legal processes and the requirements to evict tenants in the event that it is necessary. Every jurisdiction has its own regulations regarding eviction notices and timeframes and court procedures. It is important to adhere to the law to ensure your landlord rights and respect the rights of tenants.

But, keep in mind that the laws and regulations may differ greatly depending on where you live, which is why it is essential to do extensive research and seek out assistance from a professional to ensure that you're in compliance to all legal obligations within your investment sector.

Finding the Right Rental Property:

The right rental property is the most important aspect of your career as an investor in rental properties. You must take into consideration several factors in order to determine if the property is in line with the goals of your investment, and also yields desired returns.

Below are some important factors to take into consideration when looking for the perfect rental property

Placement: The place for the property rental is among of the primary elements to be considered. Consider areas with a strong rent demand with low vacancy rates as well as the potential for appreciation in the future.

Take into consideration the location's proximity to amenities, such as malls, schools or public transportation. Also, consider work centers, since they can be a draw for tenants.

Market Research Conduct a thorough market study in order to better understand local dynamics of the rental market. Study the rates of rental, vacancy as well as projected and historical increases in the population as well as economic indicators. This will allow you to assess the possibility of rental income and overall value of the investment.

The type and size of the property Select the size and type of property rental that best fits the investment strategy you are using. There are many options for single-family homes condos, multi-family homes townhouses, townhouses or commercial property. Take into consideration factors like maintaining requirements, scalability rent demand and finance options when you choose the type of property.

Conditions and maintenance: Examine the overall condition of the house. Consider whether important repairs or upgrades require consideration and the cost associated with it. A house in good condition may require a lower upfront investment and costs for maintenance.

Potential Cash Flow: Determine the cash flow potential of the property that is rented by taking into account the rental revenue and expenditures. The rental earnings are compared to tax payments on mortgages, property taxes as well as insurance, maintenance fees as well as property management charges (if appropriate) as well as all other expenditures. Cash flow that is positive and steady is usually desired, however it is important to analyze the local market and decide on a amount of cash flow according to your investment plan.

Financing Options: Consider the financing options that fit your personal financial needs and investment needs. Find out about the mortgage rate as well as down payment requirements, the terms of loans, as well as conditions for eligibility. Knowing your options for financing can help you assess the financial viability and cost of renting the property.

The Exit Strategy and Investment Goals Determine your goals for investing in terms of an accumulation of wealth in the long term as well as regular cash flow or a mixture of both. Consider your exit strategy for example, selling the home to earn a profit, or using the property for investment goals in the near future.

Professional Help: You might want to consider using real property agents, property managers or investment advisers with expertise on markets in the area. They are able to provide you with valuable information and access to properties that are not on the market as well as help you navigate the purchasing process with greater efficiency.

Take note of the fact that choosing the best rental property is a process of thorough investigation, analysis, and careful evaluation of your goals for investment. Be patient, do your the necessary due diligence and obtain the advice of a professional to make educated choices that are in line with your investment strategies.

Rental Application Process:

If you are planning to become a rental property investor within the United States, understanding the renting application procedure is essential. This involves reviewing possible tenants to locate competent and trustworthy individuals who are able to live in your rental.

Below is the guideline for the application for rental:

Create an Application for Rent: Make a complete rental application form that gathers important information from potential tenants.

Here's an example of an application for rental that is suitable for use to apply for rental in the United States.

Rental Application Form

Property   Address:

_____

Applicant Information:

Full   Name:

_____

Date   of   Birth:

_____

Phone   Number:

_____

Email   Address:

_____

Current   Address:

_____

City:

_____

___

State: _____

ZIP Code: _____

Employment Information:

Current   Employer:

_____

Position/Title:

_____

Employer's   Address:

_____

City: _____

State: _____

ZIP Code: _____

Phone Number: _____

Monthly   Income:

_____

Length   of   Employment:

_____

Former Employer (if appropriate):

Employer: _____

Position/Title: _____

Length of Employment: _____

Rental History:

Current Landlord/Property Manager:
_____

Phone Number:
_____

Previous Landlord/Property Manager:
_____

Phone Number:
_____

Personal References:

Reference 1: _____

Relationship:
_____

Phone Number:
_____

Reference 2: _____

Relationship:
_____

Phone   Number:

_____

Emergency Contact:

Name:

_____

Relationship:

_____

Phone   Number:

_____

Additional Information:

Did you have the experience of being evicted from a rental house? Yes / No

If   yes,   please   provide   details:

_____

_____

_____

Do you own pets? Yes / No

If   so,   provide   the   following   specifics:

_____

_____

__

Additional Comments or Information:

_____

_____

_____

Consent and Authorization:

I authorize the property manager to confirm the details that I have provided on this application for rental and conduct background checks, credit check, and contact with reference and employer to verify the information.

Signature: _____

Date: _____

Examine and verify applications Read through each rental application. Get in touch with the applicant's employer for verification of the income and employment information. Talk to previous landlords for information about applicants' rent history, reliability, and their payment background. In addition, you can contact personal references for a better knowledge of applicants' qualities and their suitability for tenants.

Conduct credit and background checks Get written permission from applicants for credit and background checks.

They help to determine the applicant's criminal background in addition to their creditworthiness and security. Use reputable screening companies to ensure that you are compliant with relevant legislation, including those governed by the Fair Credit Reporting Act (FCRA).

Evaluation of Applicant's Suitability: Assess the candidates based on data gathered, which includes stable employment, a steady income as well as rent history, references and creditworthiness. Take into consideration your choosing a tenant, for example your income-to-rent ratio as well as credit score and rent history. Make sure you use an equal and uniform set of criteria to prevent any discrimination.

Notify selected applicants and lease agreement: When you've found suitable applicants, you must inform the applicants of your choice. They will be provided with an agreement on lease that outlines the conditions and terms of the rental agreement, such as the price of rent and lease term, the security deposit, maintenance requirements as well as any other conditions or rules. Make sure the lease agreement is in compliance with local regulations and laws.

The procedure for moving in is to schedule a date for moving in and carry out an extensive move-in inspection of the tenants. Record the state of the property as well as any issues or damages that are present. Give tenants copies of the moving-in inspection report. Discuss the need for repairs or maintenance prior to their arrival. take over the rental.

Lease Agreements and Negotiations:

The understanding of lease agreements and negotiation is crucial to ensure the successful management of your property. Lease agreements are an legally binding agreement that specifies the terms and condition of the lease agreement between landlord and tenant.

These are the most important points to help you understand the lease agreement and negotiate:

Lease Agreement Components A typical lease contract comprises the following essential elements:

Parties involved: Make clear the names of both the landlord(s) as well as the tenant(s) that are parties to the arrangement, and the contact details for them.

Property Description: Give a full description of your rental property. This includes the address, unit's number (if relevant) as well as any other specific characteristics or amenities.

Lease Term: Indicate the term of the lease and whether it's a set term (e.g. one year) or a month-tomonth arrangement. Define the beginning and ending dates for the lease.

Rental and payment terms Be clear about the amount of rent per month as well as the date of due and acceptable ways of payments. Include information on late fees, grace period and penalties in the event of non-payment.

Security Deposit: Describe the sum of the security deposit as well as the conditions of it to be refunded, as well as any deductions to be made in the event of damages other than normal wear and wear and.

Maintenance and Repairs: Define what the roles of the tenant and landlord in regards to repairs and maintenance. Define who is accountable for particular tasks for regular maintenance, repairs due to the negligence of tenants or repair work for serious structural problems.

Utility and Service: Indicate what utilities and services are part of the rent. This includes gas, water, electricity garbage collection, and so on. If some utilities aren't specified, describe the tenant's duty to arrange and pay for these services.

Guidelines and Rules: List all rules, regulations or guidelines that tenants have to follow, like the restriction on noise levels, pets or smoking. Also, make any necessary changes in the building. Be sure to ensure that the rules adhere to local regulations and laws.

Renewal or Termination: Outline the lease renewal procedures or cancellation. Indicate any notice requirements by either side and the requirements that may lead to the early termination of a lease.

The Negotiating Lease Terms: When you are negotiating lease terms, take into consideration the following aspects:

Rent Amount: Establish the most competitive rent rate on research into the market and the local market trends. Take into consideration factors like area, property condition facilities, demand, and location in determining the amount of rent.

Lease Term: Select the most appropriate lease term which is compatible with your goals for investment. Longer-term leases can provide security and steady cash flow and a short-term lease allows for flexibility in potential rent hikes.

Responsibility for Maintenance: Define what the respective responsibilities are for the tenant and landlord in relation to repair and maintenance. Make any arrangements specific to needs from the tenant for example, shared maintenance or specific arrangements regarding the maintenance of your property.

Animal Policy: If your company is interested in allowing pets to live with you be sure to include any limitations such as additional deposits, specific rules for pets in your lease contract. Be sure to comply to local regulations as well as insurance regulations.

Modifications or improvements: Consider your position on the tenant's request for enhancements or changes to your property. Think about whether you're open to accepting modifications and if so, in what circumstances.

Early Termination: Review the terms and implications for early ending. Discuss the penalties and requirements like notice period or financial responsibility should either of the parties wants to terminate the lease earlier.

Contracts and leases will help you establish clearly defined expectations as well as protecting the rights of a rental property owner. But, as with the other guidelines mentioned earlier be aware that every state and city could have their own specific laws and regulations that govern lease contracts, and it's essential to be familiar with the laws and regulations applicable to the locality in which you're investing. Goodluck!

Financial Considerations:

Considerations regarding finances play an essential part in deciding whether to invest in rental properties across the United States. Before you invest, it's crucial to determine your financial capacity, which includes the budget you have set, your funds available for reserves and down payments and the ability to get the financing. When investing, considerations regarding finances include evaluating potential rental revenue and cash flow as well as expenses as well as profitability, to guarantee an ongoing return on investment.

This is a little more information regarding the significance of financial considerations

Before you invest in any way:

Make a Budget: Assess your financial position and decide what you're able to spend to purchase the rental of a property. Think about the money you can afford to pay for your down payment the closing cost, as well as any future renovation or repair.

Financing: Look into the options for financing, like loans or mortgages to evaluate your borrowing capability. Find out about rate of interest, loan terms and eligibility criteria for determining the viability of financing your venture.

Cash Reserves: Examine your capacity to keep reserve funds for expenses that are unexpected or periods of empty. It's essential to maintain an emergency fund to pay for repair, maintenance, management costs, as well as potential gap in income.

ROI (ROI) It is vital to the growth and longevity of your enterprise. Make sure you calculate the possible ROI by taking into account aspects like the rental income, operating expenses (property taxes and insurance costs, as well as maintenance) and the possibility of appreciation. This helps to assess the viability and profitability of your investment.

Considerations to make when investing:

Rental Income: Continuously assess the rental market and modify rent rates so that you can maximize your earnings potential. Take into consideration factors like market rent, rental rates that are comparable as well as the condition of the property and facilities when determining rent.

Cash Flow: Continuously track and analyze the cash flow produced by your rental property. Review the rental revenue against expenses such as mortgage payment tax, insurance, property taxes costs for maintenance, the cost of managing your property. Make sure you have a positive cash flow to be sure that the property earns earnings above the cost of.

Cost Management: Use cost-effective strategies for managing your expenses for reducing costs and increasing profits. Get quotes from insurance companies that are competitive for coverage. Conduct regular inspections of the property to spot the signs of deterioration early as well as look for cost-effective options for improvements and repairs.

ROI Analysis: Continuously analyze the ROI to evaluate the performance of your property. Take into consideration factors like rent yield, appreciation potential and general market conditions to decide if modifications or refinancings are required in order to maximize the financial return.

Based on my own experience, I am confident in telling you that if you carefully consider factors that affect your finances prior to and when the process of investing, you are able to make educated decisions, minimize risk, and increase the benefits you get from renting your property within the United States.

Working with landlords and property Managers:

In my time as a solicitor and intermediary to a number of clients I came to the moment that in dealing with landlords or property managers when I was a rental property owner across the United States, it's important to build a positive and efficient communications and keep an effective relationship.

This is a selection of most effective practices dealing with interactions with property managers.

Set clear expectations: clearly share your expectations with regard to the management of your property and relations with tenants. Talk about your goals for investing as well as your preferred method of communicating and any demands or needs you might are a potential investor.

Regular communication: Keep in regular and regular communication with your Property manager or landlord. Keep informed about property-related issues like maintenance concerns tenant issues, tenant complaints, as well as lease renewals. Be prompt in addressing any issues or questions that you might have, and ask for clarification if required.

Respect professional boundaries: Be aware that property managers and landlords each have responsibilities and roles. Consider their experience and make decision-making regarding managing properties including tenant selection as well as leasing administration. Don't micromanage them and allow them to perform their tasks effectively.

Make sure that you give current and accurate details to your landlord or the property manager. This could include any modifications to your contact details, changes to the plans for your investment in rental properties as well as any legal or financial issues related to your property.

Collaboration on Tenant Selection Work with your landlord or property manager on the selection of tenants. Be clear about your criteria for tenants for the requirements for creditworthiness, income verification and requirements for rental history.

Financial Management: Be informed regarding the financial aspect of the rental property you own. Review the rent collection process and review financial statements and answer any questions or concerns about expenses, income or financial statements.

Establish a professional relationship: Develop a professional and positive connection with the property's tenant or property manager. Be respectful and respond to their needs and concerns and acknowledge their work in the management of your property.

It is important to remember to ensure that you communicate effectively as well as mutual respect and cooperation are essential for landlords and property manager. If you maintain a professional connection with your property manager, you are able to work in order to guarantee the smooth running and the success of your investment in rental properties within the United States.

Moving In and Moving Out:

The process of moving from and into tenants or owners of your rental house involves careful planning, precise communication and adhering to laws. Below are some guidelines to think about:

Let's take a look at this carefully; Before moving in:

Preparing the Property: Prior to when the tenant is allowed to move in make sure the house is well-maintained and clean and in conformity with safety guidelines. Perform a thorough inspection prior to the move-in taking note of the condition of the home, and take care of any needed repairs or maintenance.

The Lease Agreement as well as the Documentation A detailed lease agreement which clarifies the conditions and terms of the lease. Make sure that both parties read and confirm the lease contract and then provide the tenant with a copy to keep for documentation. Also, collect all the needed documentation, like the identification of your tenant, income verification as well as contact information to record.

Walkthrough and Orientation: Plan an appointment with the tenant so that they are familiar with the building. Discuss how the various appliances and systems work Highlight any key features as well as provide details on how to maintain the property, connections to utilities as well as emergency contact numbers. Be sure to address any issues or questions that the customer could be facing.

Rent and Security Deposit Invoice the security deposit as well as the rent for the first month before the tenant is moved into. Make clear the payment options as well as the due dates and late payment policy. Give the tenant the receipt to keep to keep for their records.

What do you think about moving out, Let's talk about it in the following paragraphs in addition:

Communication and Notice: Create an explicit procedure for tenants to give notice of their intent to leave, in accordance with the terms stated in the lease contract. Be sure to communicate openly all through the process to resolve any concerns or questions that the tenant might need to address.

Moving Out Inspection: Plan an inspection for the move-out tenant prior to their departure. Examine the state of the house, then review it with the moving-in report and note any wear and wear and tear. The inspection can help decide the amount that will be taken in the event of a deduction of the deposit to fund repairs or for cleaning.

Security Deposit Return: Stick to legal guidelines regarding the timing and method of refunding the security deposits. If there are deductions give the tenant an exact list of deductions, along with any other supporting documents. The remainder of the security deposits promptly.

lease termination and documentation When the tenant leaves to the new location, end the lease in writing, as well as update any pertinent paperwork. Conduct a last review of the utility and services and ensure that any needed transfer or cancellations are managed in a timely manner.

Cleaning and ready the property to be rented out by the new tenant. Perform any needed repairs or maintenance needed to bring the property back to the original state. You may want to consider refreshing the property using the necessary touches-ups, cleaning and professional staging if necessary.

Advertising and Tenant Search Advertise the property and bring in prospective tenants. Change your online listings, make use of websites for rental, and utilize local media to locate the most suitable tenants. Check prospective tenants' references carefully for a reliable and trustworthy tenant of your home.

If you follow these tips in the previous paragraphs, you will be able to streamline your process for moving into and out of the rental property you own, keep an excellent landlord-tenant relationship and make sure that there is that the transition is smooth between tenants.

Tips for a Positive Rental Experience:

In order to ensure a great renter experience both for you, the landlord, and the tenants you are renting to, consider applying the following suggestions:

Clare and Complete Communication Open and Transparent Communication: Create transparent and open communication with tenants. Be clear about expectations, rules and procedures right at the outset. Quickly respond to queries or concerns and keep up-to-date with any changes that are needed.

Reliable Maintenance and Repairs Prioritize prompt and efficient management of repairs and maintenance requests. Set up a solid system for making reports on issues, and swiftly deal with them and solve these issues. Maintain the property regularly in order to avoid minor issues becoming major issues.

Respect Privacy of Tenants: Be respectful of the privacy rights of your tenants and comply with legal obligations. Give them a reasonable warning prior to accessing the property to conduct inspections, repairs or any other reasons that are necessary other than circumstances of emergency.

Affordable and consistent rent Policies Use reasonable and uniform rent policies. Do not increase rent too much give adequate notice of any change in rent and follow the local regulations on rent control when they are applicable. Be fair to all tenants and without distinction.

Rapid Rental Collection and Documentation Be clear about the expectations of rent payment as well as due dates. Make payment choices that are convenient like web-based portals and automated system. Make sure you keep exact record of rental payments and give receipts for every payment.

Routine Property Inspections Perform regular inspections of the property to verify that the lease is in compliance and to identify any safety or maintenance issues. Tenants should be given a sufficient amount of warning prior to the inspection, and take the time to resolve any concerns or to discuss repairs needed.

Conduct a thorough examine prospective tenants in order to locate honest and trustworthy people. Conduct background checks, confirm earnings and employment, and seek references from previous landlords. This increases the chance of finding tenants that are respectful of the property and meet the obligations they have.

Fast Security Deposit Handling Follow local regulations regarding the handling of security deposits. Record the condition of the property prior to the move-in date, perform inspections at the time of departure and make sure that the security deposit is returned promptly after deducting all legitimate costs related to repairs or cleaning.

Respectful and professional approach: Keep a professional and courteous behavior towards tenants. You should be courteous, respectful and prompt in all your interaction with tenants. Answer questions and complaints promptly and treat your tenants with dignity and respect.

With these suggestions to ensure an enjoyable renting experience for your tenants minimize conflicts and miscommunications as well as create an environment that is mutually beneficial and ensures a long-lasting tenant's satisfaction and long-term retention.

Chapter 2: Types Of Rental Properties & Their Benefits

Types of Rental Properties Available For Investment Purposes

When you're a landlord located in the United States, you have different types of rental property you can choose from. These are a few of the more popular ones and a short description of each one:

1. Single-Family Homes

They are houses that have been intended for one family or family. Homes that are single-family offer the benefit of privacy, and are often appealing to tenants who want higher level of residential living.

A few of the benefits include:

* Call to tenants with long-term leases looking for a place to live.

* Possibility of stable constant rental income.

• Easier management of property when in comparison to bigger multi-unit homes.

2. Multi-Family Properties

They are made up of several units within a single structure or complex. Some examples include triplexes, duplexes as well as quadplexes and apartments. Multi-family homes offer the possibility of higher rental yields as well as the benefit of economies of scale.

A few of the benefits include:

• Potential for higher rent because of several units.

* Efficiency for property management and maintenance.

• Diversified stream of income thanks to many tenants.

3. Condominiums (Condos)

Condos are privately owned units inside a building, or communities. These are usually equipped with amenities including gyms, pools and common spaces. Condos are a great investment as they offer the opportunity to own a property and also rent income.

A few of the benefits include:

* Mix of rental and ownership revenue possibility.

• Access to various amenities like pools, gyms and common spaces.

There is a possibility of less responsibility for maintenance as compared to single-family houses.

4. Townhouses

Townhouses are generally multi-level connected dwellings which share walls with units that are adjacent to them. They offer a compromise between the living space that a single-family house offers and the less frequent maintenance of condominiums or apartments.

The benefits of this also are:

* A balance between the size of a single-family house and the less maintenance for condos.

* Call for tenants who want an increase in privacy and an underlying sense of belonging.

* Possibility of stable rental income as well as long-term.

5. Vacation Rentals

They are specifically advertised to vacationers who require short-term rental. These could be homes condominiums, apartments, or condos situated in tourist areas that are popular. The rental market for vacation rentals is usually higher in rentals during the peak season however they may also incur higher running expenses.

A few of the benefits include:

• Potentially higher rent in peak season.

The flexibility to utilize the house for private vacations.

• Tax-free advantages associated with renting short-term properties.

Student Housing

Property near schools and colleges which cater to students renting. Housing for students can take the form of homes for single families apartment buildings, multi-unit properties. The investment in this type comes from the steady need for accommodation for students.

A few of the benefits include:

Demand of student accommodations near college and universities.

Possibility of more rental income when there are multiple tenants.

The lower vacancy rate is because of a steady students.

6. Commercial Properties

The category covers properties that include commercial buildings, retail spaces warehouses, industrial property. The investment into commercial real estate may guarantee long-term stable tenants and potential higher yields, however it typically requires more money and experience.

A few of the benefits include:

* Long-term, stable tenants with leases for commercial properties.

Potentially better returns when as compared to residential property.

* Diversification of income by diverse commercial tenants.

7. Mobile Homes

Mobile homes or manufactured houses are homes that have been prefabricated at a factory before being delivered to specific locations. The purchase of mobile homes could bring lower prices as well as affordable housing options to tenants.

A few of the benefits include:

Lower entry cost when compared with traditional types of housing.

A low-cost housing solution for renters.

The potential for a greater rental returns because of the lower cost of purchase.

8. Mixed-Use Properties

They are properties that include commercial and residential areas within the same structure or in a complex. As an example, a structure could have apartment units on top floors as well as offices or retail spaces on the ground. Mixed-use buildings can provide a variety of revenue streams and serve different tenants.

Its benefits are:

The diversification of the income from both commercial and residential tenants.

* Possibility for more rental income from a variety of sources.

• Convenient facilities and services available to residents of the same complex or building.

8. Single-Room Rentals

They are also known as boarding homes or rooms, these houses let out spaces to renters.

One-room rentals are typically cheaper for tenants, and may be a good investment option in specific locations that have the highest demand.

Its benefits are:

A low-cost housing solution that allows tenants to rent at lower cost.

* Possibility for better rental return when renting individual rooms.

* Flexibility to accommodate various requirements of tenants and budgets.

But, it is vital to do your research thoroughly and conduct feasibility studies to find out the type of rental property that best suits your investment objectives and local market conditions and your individual preferences as a potential investor.

Each kind of property has specific considerations and problems, which is why it's important to take into consideration factors like property location, demand for rentals as well as the requirements for property management as well as potential rental income, in making investment choices.

Be aware that the pros and cons of every type of rental property depend on factors like the location, market conditions, demands from tenants and individual investment goals. You must carefully think about the factors that affect you and carry out an exhaustive market analysis prior to taking any investment decision.

Chapter 3: The Factors That Influence Rental Rates

Many factors influence price of rental and accessibility of homes for landlord. These are the most important factors to think about:

1. Its location: The area of a home is among the major factors that affect the cost of renting and its availability. Locations that are convenient with infrastructure, excellent schools as well as employment possibilities, and accessibility to public transportation are likely to attract higher rents. In addition, in

areas that are highly sought-after the area may have few properties available that are available for rental, which can lead to an increase in competition among tenants.

2. Situation of the Market: general condition of the market for real estate will affect rental rates as well as the availability of properties. In a highly competitive market, with a high demand and low supply, prices for rental will likely be more expensive and availability of rental homes could be restricted. However, in a slower market that has less competition, rent prices could be less and, in turn, there will be a greater number of properties available to lease.

3. The type of property and the size: A variety of sizes and types of properties may have different rental rates and supply. In particular, bigger properties like multi-unit structures or single-family houses generally have higher rental costs compared to smaller properties such as studios and one-bedroom units. There are a variety of property kinds can vary based

upon the market in your area and the zoning rules.

4. Facilities and Condition of the Property Facilities and Condition of a rental home will affect the rental cost as well as its appeal to prospective tenants. Properties that are well-maintained and have desirable amenities like modern kitchens, new appliances, washers and dryers in units parking, as well as outside spaces will attract higher rents and draw more renters.

5. The Local Economic Impact: Local economic and social conditions in a particular area influence pricing of rentals and the availability of properties. A strong job market, expansion of the population, as well as growth in the economy can raise rent demand, which can result in increased rental costs. However, economic slowdowns or job losses could lead to a decline in demand for rental and lower rents.

6. Costs of Landlords: Landlords take into account their expenditures, like the cost of

mortgages, property taxes and insurance costs, maintenance expenses and utility bills, in determining rental rates. The higher costs could result in more expensive rental rates to guarantee the profitability of. But landlords should also take into account competition from the market and the willingness of tenants to pay for those rates.

7. Government Regulations: State and local government regulations, such as lease control laws and tenant protection laws zoning regulations, as well as licensing rules, may affect rent prices as well as property availability. They could impact the ability of landlords to raise rent or alter the general rent market's dynamics.

8. Demographic Factors like the growth of population, earnings, and the lifestyle of individuals, may affect rent prices as well as the availability of property. Regions that are experiencing a rapid increase in population as well as a large need for housing rental may see higher rents as well as limited supply.

9. Seasonal Demand: Seasonal conditions may affect the rental price as well as availability of property, particularly those in tourist destinations and student-centric regions. Price increases may occur in peak times as demand rises as well as availability could be restricted due to the an increase in competition.

It is crucial for investors in rental properties to consider these elements and undertake thorough market research in order to learn about local market dynamics and take informed choices about pricing for rental properties and the availability of property.

Benefits and purpose of this book are:

First, The Purpose:

The goal of this guide is to equip prospective investors looking to invest in rental properties within the United States with a comprehensive information that will help them take informed decisions and ensure the success they desire in their real estate endeavors. This book is tailored specifically to the needs of investors in the rental market who seek practical tips as well as strategies in order to navigate the property rental market efficiently.

The main goals are:

Empowerment and Education: The publication aims to teach and empower renters through providing them with the necessary information and knowledge of the market for rental properties. The book covers a variety of topics of the analysis of market conditions, choosing a property and financing alternatives and legal issues as well as property management and maximising yields.

Complete Guidance This book presents an approach that is step-by-step, guiding viewers through the complete rental process, starting beginning with initial research and acquisition through management of tenants as well as long-term financial viability. It covers the essential aspects and nuances of investing in rental properties in an easy-to-understand method.

Practical Tips and Strategies With a focus on practicality this book provides renters with tried and true methods, strategies and the best ways to overcome challenges, maximize rent income, reduce risk, and create an effective rental portfolio. The book provides insights on effective managing property, tenant screening lease contracts, improving the experience of tenants.

Market Insights: Understanding and recognizing the significance of understanding the dynamics of markets this book offers important insight into the rental property market across the United States. It examines trends in the market as well as local variations in market prices as well as factors that influence rental rates so that readers can decide based on data the specific areas they want to target.

Problems and Pitfalls to Avoid Understanding the fact that investing in rental properties may have its fair share of difficulties, this book outlines the most common mistakes and offers advice in how to get around the challenges. The book covers topics like security management, maintenance of the property and dealing with tenants who are difficult and adjusting to changes in the market.

Practical Examples from the Real World and Case Studies to help improve knowledge, the book contains actual examples and case studies which illustrate the most important concepts and show successful ways to invest in rental property.

These scenarios highlight various possibilities that include investment options, strategies, and results. They provide readers with useful information and motivation.

Resources Compilation: Recognizing importance of other resources The book provides an assortment of suggested tools, sites, software as well as other information sources that renters can use to conduct further analysis, research as well as support.

In the end, the goal of this guide is to equip rental investors with the information about strategies, techniques, and trust needed to navigate through the complexities of investing in rental properties effectively. Through providing them with necessary tools and knowledge in order to assist to attain the financial objectives they have set, create the wealth of real estate and finally, to create a rewarding and enjoyable renting property experience.

How Much On The Average One Can Use To Start A Rental Investment In The United States As Of Today

The amount needed to begin a rental venture within the United States can vary significantly according to various variables like area, the type of property markets, conditions of the market, as well as the individual goals of investment.

There are some general estimations of what the standard cost involved in this for you They are not in any particular order. I have listed them below:

1. The Down Payment: If you're buying an investment property for rental it is common to pay a down payment which can be a proportion of the price paid for the property. The amount you pay for a down payment could vary from 15 to 25 percent of the value. In the example above, if you're looking at a home valued at $200,000, a amount of 20% could be equivalent to the equivalent of $40,000.

2. Close Costs in addition to the cost of a down cost, there are a variety of closing costs that are associated with purchasing an investment house. They include charges for property appraisals as well as inspections, title search as well as loan origination and legal fees. In the average, closing costs vary between 2% and 5 percent of the cost of purchase. If a property is worth $200,000 the

closing cost could range from between $4,000 and $10,000.

3. Renovations and repairs Based on the state of the house it may be necessary make provision for changes or renovations in order to allow it to rent. The cost will be depending on the amount of the work to be done as well as the level you want to improvements.

4. Property Management Fees are planning to employ an agency to manage your property and manage the day-to-day operation of your rental property it is important to consider the charges.

Management fees for properties usually vary from 8% to 12percent of rent earned each month.

Other Expenses: There are various miscellaneous expenses that you should consider including tax on property and insurance premiums, regular repair and maintenance, advertising expenditures as well as vacancy expenses. They can differ based upon the area and size of the building.

It is important to be aware that the numbers provided are rough estimates that could differ significantly based on particular unforeseen circumstance. It is recommended to speak with an experienced real estate agent or financial adviser to get an accurate estimate in line with your goals for investment as well as the market conditions in your local area.

Furthermore, financial options for example, like getting an mortgage can drastically decrease the amount of initial capital required. But, it's important to evaluate the financial consequences that a loan can bring and think about the potential dangers and liabilities.

Chapter 4: 25 Hidden Secrets Experts Are Using To Make Profit In The Industry

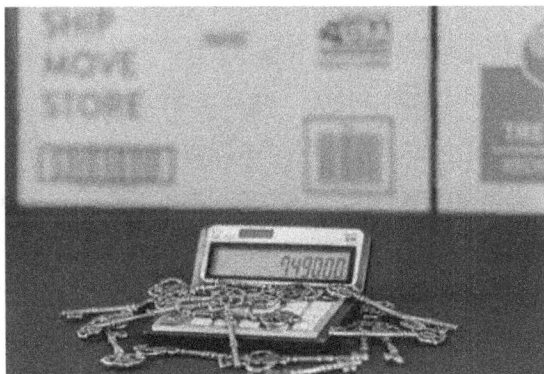

The Hidden Secrets

In the case of investing in rental properties within the United States, there are many secrets experts employ to increase profits. These are the most important tips which newbies might not have a clue about.

A thorough market research: Successful investors carry out extensive research in order to find markets that have high rental demand as well as positive economic circumstances. They take into account factors such as increasing population size, the job market and rental vacancy rates as well as future plans for development.

Property Location: Selecting the best location for your property is essential. It is recommended to look for communities with desirable amenities such as shopping centres, schools transport access, lower crime rates. Additionally, they look at their proximity to major employment centers and the possibility of future growth.

The Cash Flow Analyse: Professionals know the value of performing an extensive cash flow analysis prior making a decision to invest. The analysis includes all expenditures like mortgage payment and property taxes and insurance costs, maintenance expenses and vacancies as well as property administration fees. A positive cash flow is an important indicator of an investment property that is profitable.

Financial Strategies for Investors: Experienced investors look at various financing strategies for maximizing their profits. They could leverage methods including creative financing, like private lending, partnerships or seller financing in order to cut down on the initial cost and maximize the potential profit.

Property Management: Effective property management is essential for the long-term viability of your property. Experts frequently employ professional firms to manage rental screening for tenants maintenance, repairs and more. Investors can focus on purchasing more properties, and also ensures smoother operation.

Tenant screening: Finding trustworthy and accountable tenants is crucial. The best experts implement strict tenant screening procedures, which include the use of credit checks, verification of employment as well as rental history verification as well as background screening. This reduces the chance of a problematic tenant and the possibility of problems later on.

A proper insurance coverage: Proper insurance protection protects investors against unpredictable events such as the possibility of liability or property damage. Insurance professionals are experts that specialize in rental homes to be sure that they have the right coverage for their particular needs.

Tax Benefits: Knowing the tax benefits of the rental property can greatly impact the profitability of your rental property. Experts collaborate with knowledgeable accountants and tax experts in order to maximize deductions, including depreciation and repairs, maintenance expenses and mortgage interest.

Long-Term Appreciation: Investors who are successful tend to focus on homes with the possibility of long-term appreciation. They study historical market trends and local plans for development as well as infrastructure upgrades to pinpoint regions that are likely to grow. This approach can result in an increase in property value and better return on investment.

Continued Education and Networking Experts also stress the importance of continuous training and networking in the real estate sector. attending workshops or joining real estate investment associations, and establishing contacts with experienced investors may offer valuable information and potential to grow.

Experts use leverage to increase appreciation in property by carefully refinancing or taking out home equity loans in order to buy other homes. This lets them increase their investments, and improve the value of their portfolio overall.

Value-Add Opportunities: seasoned investors look for properties that have potential value-add. They seek out properties that are able to be upgraded by renovations, upgrades or strategies for repositioning. In addition, adding value boosts rent income as well as the property's value which results in better returns.

Negotiation skills: It skills play an important role in the field of real estate investment. Professionals develop their skills in negotiation to obtain an acceptable purchase price or financing terms as well as contractors' rates. The ability to negotiate successfully could result in substantial reduction in costs and higher profits.

Exit Strategies: Those who are successful have their exit strategies planned ahead of time. They look at options for selling the property at an income, refinancing the property to gain equity and converting from short-term rentals into long-term leases. A clear exit strategy ensures investors get the most out of the market and earn maximum return.

Understanding Rent Trends Experts keep themselves informed regarding trends in rental rates within the markets they are targeting. They look at rental information and market dynamics in order to decide the most efficient rent rates. With competitive rents that attract good tenants and limit vacancies and maximize the potential for income.

A Reliable Team A reliable team is vital to the success of. Experts work with experts including real estate agents contractors, property managers and lawyers that specialize in the rental of properties. The team offers valuable advice as well as support and knowledge through the whole investing process.

Continuous learning and adaptation: Real estate changes constantly. The experts are aware of the need for continuing learning and adjusting in order to stay on top. They constantly research emerging strategies, market trends as well as emerging markets for making informed decisions about investments.

Diversification of the Investment portfolio is an important approach for professionals. They are able to invest in a variety of kinds of properties (single-family houses, multi-unit structures commercial property) and also diversify their portfolios across different areas to limit risks and take advantage of opportunities in various sectors.

Planning for vacant spaces: Professionals are able to anticipate vacant positions and prepare according to. Reserves are set aside to pay for costs during vacant times, perform regular maintenance to attract tenants as well as implement strategies for marketing to reduce the time between tenants.

Long-Term Mindset: Successful investors adopt a long-term mindset. They realize the importance of real estate as an investment that is long-term and they focus on creating a portfolio that is sustainable. This helps them endure market volatility and profit of long-term appreciation as well as cash flow.

Becoming aware of legal and Regulatory Updates Experts keep themselves updated with the laws of both federal and local jurisdictions and laws governing rentals. They make sure that the property is in conformity to fair housing laws as well as landlord-tenant rules and security codes. This will help you avoid legal trouble and expensive penalties.

Energy Efficiency and Sustainability: Progressive investors are focusing on energy efficiency and sustainability. They make investments in energy efficient appliances in the form of insulation, smart technology to cut running costs as well as attract eco responsible tenants.

Calculating the Return On Investment (ROI) Experts take time to evaluate ROI of each property. They look at the flow of cash and possible equity growth in order to determine the investment's potential profitability. Being aware of ROI allows them to prioritize those properties that offer the best potential return.

Protection from Risk: Professionals take care to reduce risks in renting properties. They are covered by insurance and have a strict lease agreement and conduct periodic inspections of the property as well as maintain solid reserves in the financial department to cope with any unexpected circumstances.

Continuous Evaluation and Optimization of Portfolios: Investors who are experienced regularly assess the performance of their portfolios and adjust their portfolios as necessary. They can sell property that is not performing or refinance in order to improve cash flow, or shift funds to areas that have higher chance of growth.

Chances Of Getting High ROI On Rental Properties By Foreigners Like Their United States Investors Counterparts In The Line Of Same Business in The United States

Foreign investors are sure to find satisfaction in the rental property industry in the United States. Although there are particular challenges and concerns that foreigners face however, the field is usually level and the opportunities are there for international investors. These are the most important points to think about:

Property ownership: Investors from abroad have the legal right to invest and own in rental properties within the United States. There are no limits or restrictions based on citizenship.

Finance Options: Foreign investors are able to access a range of funding options within the U.S., including traditional mortgages, private lender and partnerships. But, it is crucial to keep in mind that the requirements for financing could vary depending on the non-U.S. citizen. Investors from outside the United States may have more documentation or satisfy specific eligibility requirements.

Knowledge of the local market: A major issue for investors from abroad is to gain a thorough understanding about the market in their local area. It is essential to research thoroughly and comprehend the nuances of the particular region or city that they are planning to make investments. Working with local experts, like real estate agents and property managers can give important insights into market trends regulation, potential investment options.

Tax implications: Investors from abroad need to be aware of U.S. tax regulations, which are often complex. It is highly recommended that foreign investors to speak with an experienced tax professional with expertise in international taxation, to be aware of the tax requirements, possible deductions and treaties that they have with their home country as well as the U.S.

Property Management: Distinction could pose a hurdle when it comes to foreign investors in the realm of managing properties. Engaging a property management service is typically suggested to oversee day-today operations as well as tenant management and maintenance of the property. It will ensure efficient management and assurance for overseas investors.

Cultural and language differences Foreign investors must be cognizant of the differences in culture and languages when doing business within America. United States. Networking, building relationships and efficient communication are essential. It is useful to partner with local agents or partners that can help make the connection and assist in easy trades.

Legal and regulatory considerations Foreign investors should be in compliance the U.S. laws and regulations regarding real estate investment as well as landlord-tenant relationship as well as fair housing and the management of property. Employing an experienced attorney who is familiar with the laws governing real estate is recommended in order to make sure that you are compliant and to avoid legal problems.

Exchange Rates and Currency Flows Foreign investors must take into consideration the exchange rate and possible fluctuation in the currency rate when making investments. They can affect the return that investors get from their investments and the flow of cash.

Risk Management: As with all investments there are risk associated to investing in rental properties. Foreign investors must evaluate and manage risk through rigorous due diligence and diversifying their portfolios and ensuring they have adequate insurance protection.

Although foreign investors could face other issues, with some analysis, planning as well as professional guidance and guidance, they will be able to establish an equal playing field and be successful on the U.S. renting property. It is crucial that foreign investors familiarize their self with the local market's rules, conditions, and good practices in order to make an informed decision about investments and reach their objectives.

What are the restrictions to the investment in rental properties within the USA

When investing in rental properties across the United States can be lucrative but it's crucial to be conscious of the risks and pitfalls that come to this particular type of investment.

Here are a few common limitations:

Market volatility Market volatility: Real estate markets may be subject to fluctuation as well as volatility. Market conditions, economic factors, local changes, as well as other factors that are that are beyond the control of an investor can affect the value of property and demand for rentals. It's crucial to prepare for market declines that could occur as well as plan the long-term strategy of investment.

The initial capital requirement for investing in rental properties usually will require a substantial amount of initial capital. In the purchase of properties, getting the financing (if necessary) and covering related expenses like down payments and closing expenses, repair costs as well as renovations could be significant obstacles for investors.

Problems with Financing: Finding finance for rental properties may be harder than homes that are primary. Some lenders have more stringent requirements in relation to investment properties. This includes more hefty down payment percentages as well as stricter credit score requirements as well as more cautious ratios between income and debt. Foreign investors might face additional obstacles when trying to obtain funding.

Property Management: managing the management of rental properties is laborious and time-consuming. Investors are required to handle the screening of tenants, collecting rent repair, maintenance of the property as well as dealing with possible conflicts or Evictions. This could require the hiring of an agency for property management and can affect the profitability of the entire business.

Potential Cash Flow and Vacancy Risks The rental properties are subject to the possibility of vacancies that could affect the cash flow.

It is important to consider the possibility of vacant periods and be sure that you have sufficient reserves in place to pay for the costs of those periods. The cost of unexpected repairs or maintenance may also have an impact on the cash flow.

Property Maintenance and Upkeep Properties that are rented require regular maintenance and repairs on occasion. These include routine chores like painting, landscaping and plumbing in addition to significant repair or replacements. It is essential for investors to set aside resources and time to maintain the property in order to draw tenants, keep them in the property and preserve the value of the property.

Legal and Regulatory Compliance Property owners who own rental properties must adhere to a variety of laws and regulations which include fair laws regarding housing, building codes Zoning regulations, the laws governing landlords and tenants. Making sure you are aware of the laws and regulations may require additional time, energy, and legal costs.

Insurance and Liability: Owning rental property comes with a certain amount of liability potential. Investors require appropriate insurance to safeguard against damage to property as well as liability claims and lawsuits. Insufficient insurance coverage could be expensive, and can affect general profitability.

Competitiveness and Market Saturation In certain areas, the market for rental properties can become overcrowded, resulting in more competition from investors. The result can have an impact on the rates of rental, vacancy rate as well as overall profit. A thorough market analysis is essential to determine areas with positive demand and supply patterns.

Economic and political factors: Political and economic factors local and nationally affect investment in rental properties. Variations in the interest rate and tax laws, as well as regulatory policies, and economic slowdowns may affect property value and financing accessibility as well as rental demand and general investment performance.

Being aware of these constraints will help investors make educated choices and devise strategies to reduce risk. Research, thorough plan, and a long-term approach are crucial to successfully navigating this hazard and increasing the chances to succeed in the rental property investment.

What are the driving aspects that will propel any investor into success when they enter this industry, regardless of color, race, or nationality within the United States?

The United States offers a favorable atmosphere for all, irrespective of race, nationality, or race, to excel when it comes to investing in rental properties. These are the key aspects that are crucial to success in the field:

A solid legal framework Strong Legal Framework: The United States has a robust legal system which protects property rights as well as an open and fair procedure for transactions in property. It allows investors, regardless of their backgrounds, to be a part of markets and have the same protections under law as well as potential.

Market Dimension and Diversity Dimensions and Diversity: The U.S. real estate market is huge and diverse and offers opportunities in a variety of areas and types of property. With its large population, an active economy and an array of demand for rental properties There are markets that can be adapted to a variety of investing strategies and styles.

Opportunities and Entrepreneurial Spirit Opportunities and Entrepreneurial Spirit: Opportunities and Entrepreneurial Spirit: United States has a strong entrepreneurial spirit and the history of ingenuity and investing opportunities. Investment in real estate is in sync with this mindset, which allows investors to create an asset, earn an income that is passive, as well as create the financial freedom they desire.

Chapter 5: Seminars, Trainings And Sponsorships

Seminars and Workshops

There are a variety of workshops and seminars available to prospective investors who want to expand their understanding of rental investment in property. These are a few of the most popular seminars:

Training for Real Estate Investors offered by FortuneBuilders: FortuneBuilders offers workshops as well as training courses that are focused on investing in real estate. They cover a variety of aspects of investing such as the search for deals, rehabilitating properties as well as building a portfolio of rental properties as well as property management.

National Real Estate Investors Association (REIA) Seminars: REIA chapters across the United States organize seminars and occasions to help educate the investors. The seminars focus on topics including financial analysis, market analysis and strategies for acquisition of property and best practices for managing property.

BiggerPockets Event: BiggerPockets, a popular online community for real estate investors hosts live events as well as conferences. They host professional speakers panels, discussions with panelists, networking opportunities and informative seminars that cover a variety of issues regarding rental property investment.

Rich Dad Education Workshops Rich Dad Education gives training and seminars in real estate investment as well as financial education. The programs offer a variety of investing strategies, which include rentals, as well as providing information on how to make money through the real estate market.

Real Estate Investor Association (REIA) Events Local REIA organizations often have regularly scheduled meetings and seminars which give valuable info and networking opportunities. The meetings are accompanied by guests speakers, education discussions, analysis of deals, as well as case studies that will increase the knowledge of investors.

Local Community College Real Estate Courses There are many community colleges that offer classes in real estate that focus on investments strategies, property analyses finance, as well as various other subjects. The courses could provide an excellent foundation for novice investors as well as help investors who are experienced expand their expertise.

Online Webinars, Virtual Summits and other webinars. Numerous companies and industry professionals offer online webinars and virtual summits to discuss renting property investment. They allow investors to gain knowledge from experts, engage in interactive Q&A sessions and get insights into certain subjects of interest.

Real Estate Investment Trust (REIT) Conferences: REIT conferences bring together professional from the field, including fund managers, investors, and analysts to talk about developments, investment strategies and market information. These conferences provide important information about the overall market for real estate investments.

real Estate Investment Groups and Meetups Local Real Estate Investment Groups and attending meetups may give you the chance to hear from experienced investors, impart experiences, and meet people who are similar to you. They often host educational seminars or events with guest speakers.

Online Learning Platforms: Websites such Udemy, Coursera, and LinkedIn Learning offer online courses as well as programs for real estate investment. The courses covered cover a broad variety of subjects, such as investment in rental properties as well as property analysis, financing as well as property management.

Be sure to investigate and assess the legitimacy and value of any event or conference before you attend. Additionally, you can seek advice from experienced investors or professional experts who've attended these events.

Where can investors turn in the event of deciding to begin or whom can they contact for guidance within the United States?

If you are thinking about the possibility of investing in rental properties within the USA Investors typically interact with various key institutions as well as professionals in order to collect data, obtain advice to begin their journey to invest. These are the key sources for investors to think about:

Real estate agents: Agents who specialize in investment properties could provide valuable information to investors. They are knowledgeable about the market and may help find the right properties that meet investment objectives locations, preferences for location, and financial budget. They are able to provide insight into the local rental market, properties value, and the potential for rent income.

Real Estate Investment Associations joining real estate investment group or local associations for real estate can provide investors with similar interests as well as experienced investors and experts in the field. They often hold meetings or seminars as well as networking events that provide the opportunity to hear from professionals and gain an understanding of the latest market changes.

Loan Brokers and Mortgage Brokers Buyers looking to finance their business may consult with lenders or mortgage brokers. These experts can assist buyers through the application process, analyze their financial standing and provide mortgage alternatives specific to their requirements. They are able to help identify the amount of loan, conditions, and rates which best meet the investor's objectives in terms of finances.

Property Management Companies: Investors who want an approach that is more hands-off or are investing in homes situated far from where they live could consider hiring firms to manage their properties. These firms specialize in managing rentals, and handling tenant selection, rental collection as well as property maintenance along with other operations.

They are able to provide invaluable advice as well as help investors understand the maze of managing property.

Real Estate Lawyers Legal counsel for real estate offer legal guidance as well as guidance during the investing process. They are able to review purchase agreements as well as lease agreements and other legal documents, and ensure that they are in compliance with local regulations and laws. Attorneys are also able to assist in establishment of an entity and asset protection strategies and in settling legal disputes when they occur.

Local Market Experts Connecting with market professionals in the local area like appraisers, inspectors, contractors and others, will provide investors with beneficial information about the state of their properties, costs for renovations and the potential for risks as well as issues that are particular to the local market.

Furthermore, investors can profit from doing their own studies, participating in conference or seminars on real estate or looking through online sources that focus on investing in real estate in the USA. The development of a social network in the investment community of real estate could lead to beneficial connections, partnerships, as well as more possibilities.

Be sure to do your due diligence and examine the credentials and knowledge of the professionals you choose, and then select the ones that align to your financial goals and beliefs.

Fears of Uncertainty By Investor

If you are considering investing into rental properties, people are likely to experience a range of worries and worries. It is important to tackle the fears in a proactive manner and to have strategies to address the potential risks. These are common concerns which investors could face and suggestions for solutions:

Beware of Financial Risks The investment in rental property has financial risks and commitments. Solution: Do a an extensive financial analysis prior to making a decision to invest.

Examine your cash flow forecasts, and possible risk. Set up a contingency account to help cover any unexpected expenses or empty positions. Think about consulting a financial professional to confirm that the investment you choose to make is in line with your risk-taking capacity and your financial objectives.

Beware of vacant properties Fear of Not having tenants to rent or suffering prolonged periods of vacantness is a daunting thought. Solution: Study the rental market in your area for a better understanding of rent and demand. Consider investing in property located in areas that have a significant rent demand. Make sure your property is maintained and is attractive to potential tenants. Think about partnering with a property management firm to manage leasing and selection.

The fear of difficult tenants The issue of dealing with difficult or not paying tenants is an issue. Solution: Use a comprehensive screening of tenants to reduce the chance of having problematic tenants. Examine applicants' credit score as well as employment as well as rental references. Make clear the terms of the lease agreement, and follow guidelines regularly. Think about landlord insurance as a way to safeguard against liability or damages that could occur.

Be afraid of property Maintenance and repairs Property maintenance as well as unexpected repairs could seem daunting. Solution: Set aside money for upkeep and repair. Regularly inspect your premises to spot the issues before they become serious. Establish relationships with trustworthy contractors and service suppliers. Think about including maintenance clauses into lease agreements in order to define tenant obligations. Consider landlord insurance that can will cover damages and repairs.

The fear of Regulatory Compliance The process of navigating local, state, and federal local regulations can be difficult. Solution: Get educated on the laws and regulations that apply to the rental property. Talk to an attorney for real estate or a Property management companies for that you are in compliance. Keep up-to-date on any changes to law and regulations that could influence the value of your property.

Beware of Market Volatility Beware of market volatility and economic recessions could be a factor. Solution: Diversify your investment portfolio to mitigate risks. Make sure you focus on investment strategies that are long-term and not on short-term market volatility. Perform thorough market research and make investments in regions with rent markets that are stable or increasing.

Afraid of Insufficient Cash Flow Fear of not having enough funds to pay for the costs and make profits can cause anxiety. Solution: Conduct a detailed analyses of finances. This includes precise estimates of the rental revenue and expenditures. Consider vacancy potential along with maintenance expenses and management charges for the property. Determine realistic rental rates in order to guarantee a steady flow of cash. Check and revise regularly rent rates in line with the market's current conditions.

Be aware that addressing your fears requires careful plan, market research, proper diligence and an active approach to managing. It's essential to constantly be educated, obtain the advice of a professional when you need it and adjust your strategy when circumstances change. If you follow these guidelines to minimize risk, you will be able to reduce the risks and boost your chances of making a profit from a renting property.

The possibilities of sponsorship to the Rental Investor In The United States Look into these.

Here are a few common choices:

Personal Savings: A lot of investors make use of their own personal savings to finance their investment in rental properties. This can include the cash reserve, equity in the properties they own, or by selling other investments in order to make capital.

Traditional banks and mortgage lenders Mortgage lenders and banks provide a variety of financing options for investment in rental properties like traditional mortgages, portfolio loans commercial loans, and portfolio loans. They assess your creditworthiness as well as the property's ability to repay in order to decide the amount of loan and its terms.

Private Lenders Private Lenders: Private lenders, whether businesses or individuals, can provide different financing options to real estate investors who want to rent their properties. They typically have greater flexible lending requirements and can be more willing to lend money on properties conventional banks might consider to be riskier.

Chapter 6: Mortgage Plans And Rental Investing

What's the connection between mortgages for home ownership and rentals?

The mortgage for homeowners as well as rental property are distinct elements of investing in real estate, however, they are connected in a variety of ways. For instance, as follows:

Finance Rental Property Purchase: Homeownership mortgages can be utilized for financing the purchase of rental homes. Investors are able to obtain an investment loan in order to buy an asset with the aim of leasing it to tenants. Mortgage lenders usually offer a range of alternatives for investment properties which might have particular terms and conditions compared to homeowner-occupied mortgages.

Cash flow generation Renting properties are typically bought as investment properties that earn income for the purpose of producing revenue from rentals that surpasses costs of the property, which includes mortgage repayments. If you can get a mortgage that is favorable to plan, property owners could get a lower monthly mortgage installment that results in greater cash flow and a higher profit through your rental home.

Equity Construction: Homeownership mortgage plans let individuals build equity in their homes in the course of some time. It can then be utilized for the purchase of other rental property. By making regular mortgage payments, as well as property appreciation homeowners are able to accumulate funds that they can tap to pay down the mortgage or for financing additional property investment.

Exit Strategies: Mortgages for homeownership and rental properties could meet when investors opt to convert a former owner-occupied home into a rental.

If, for instance, someone decides to relocate to rent out their previous property, they can either keep the mortgage they have in place or modify it to an investment mortgage for property. It allows homeowners to turn their house to a rental property which can generate income and getting the benefit of appreciation on their property.

The stability of your personal finances: Owning a home provides a feeling of financial security and provide the foundation needed to invest in real estate. With favorable mortgage terms as well as building equity in the home they live in they are more likely to be able to get loans or obtain financing for rental homes. An excellent financial standing resulting of homeownership could improve an investor's real estate portfolio as well as his potential investment options.

It's crucial to understand that although homeownership mortgages are beneficial when compared to rentals, these two notions require distinct aspects to be considered. The requirements for getting the mortgage needed for your principal residence are different from the criteria of investment properties. Likewise, investors evaluate investment properties for rental in light of factors such as the potential for rental income, the area of the property, as well as the investment's financial situation.

In the end, homeownership plans and rental properties are able to be a perfect match and allow individuals to use their wealth and stability for a larger real estate portfolio investment and possibly generate wealth over the long term.

Which are the authorities which regulate landlords and tenant right to rent properties in the United states?

The United States, landlord-tenant relationships and the rules for rental properties are generally controlled by a mix of state, federal, and local legislation.

These are the main authorities and rules involved:

Federal Laws:

Fair Housing Act (FHA) is enforced through HUD U.S. Department of Housing and Urban Development (HUD) and the FHA does not permit discrimination based on race or color or religion, sexual orientation, family status, national origin or disability, in the rental dwellings.

State Laws:

Every state has their individual regulations and laws to regulate landlord-tenant partnerships as well as rental property. A few of the most well-known regulatory bodies are:

State Housing agencies: Responsible for overseeing the affordable housing program, as well as enforcing the housing code, and offering resources to tenants and landlords.

State Attorney General's Office: Addresses legal problems and disputes relating to the laws governing landlords and tenants as well as consumer protection.

The State Real Estate Commissions Control the profession of real estate agents and offer instructions on how to manage property.

Local Laws: Cities as well as municipalities usually have rules and regulations which govern rentals. Local bodies could comprise:

Local Housing Authorities oversee the public housing program, manage rentals, as well as enforce the local housing laws.

Rent Control Boards, or Commissions found in a few cities that have rent control laws They regulate the increase in rent and protect tenants.

It's crucial to keep in mind the fact that regulations as well as rights and enforcement agencies may differ between states as well as within local authorities. It is therefore recommended that tenants and landlords be aware of the particular legislation and rules that are applicable in their particular location.

Alongside the regulatory authorities tenant and landlords could enjoy rights and protections stipulated in lease agreements or lease agreements. These contracts have legal force and define the conditions and obligations for both parties. Any disputes or violation of rights are resolved by mediation, negotiation, or through legal action, based on the seriousness and severity of the problem.

A legal consultation with an experienced attorney, or consulting local housing sources can offer additional details on legal rights and regulatory authorities that are applicable to the specific rental property within the United States.

What is the punishment in case of default or failure to follow the procedures before starting the rental business within the United States?

The consequences for defaulting on rentals property obligation or failure to adhere to the appropriate procedure prior to launching a rental investment company within the United States can vary depending upon the particular circumstances and the applicable law. Below are a few possible penalties:

Breakage of Lease Agreement: If an investor violates the terms of the lease for instance, failing to pay rent, or in violation of any other clause, the breaching person may seek legal actions. It could result in financial damages, eviction actions as well as a negative impression on the credit score of the person.

A violation of Fair Housing Laws: Discrimination in the context of protected characteristics like religion, race, color, gender, national origin as well as familial or disability, is illegal under the federal fair housing laws. Infractions could lead to investigation and penalties, fines and even litigation.

Inability to comply to the Building Codes and Safety Regulations: Renting properties have to meet specific requirements set out in the building codes and safety laws. Infractions can lead to penalty, fines, or required repairs or upgrades as well as legal action either from the landlord or the authorities.

Inappropriate or unauthorised use of Deposits in Security: Improper handling security deposit funds, including making use of them for activities prohibited by law, or not returning the funds in a timely manner, could result in legal penalties. The laws regarding security deposits differ in each state. Violations could result in fines as well as double damages or additional financial liability.

Non-licensed Property Management or Real Estate Activity: Engaging with property management or real estate-related activities that are not licensed can result in legal consequences. The state laws regulate license requirements for property management and real estate professionals or operating with no license could result in penalties or legal proceedings, as well as the possibility of being restricted from conducting business.

It's crucial to keep in mind that the penalties and repercussions differ between states and are influenced by local rules. Always recommend and secure to speak with legal experts like attorneys who specialize in property or real estate law, in order to be sure that you're complying with the laws and regulations in force prior to launching the rental investment venture.

As I've always suggested, understanding and following the correct due process and obtaining all the required permits and certificates, will aid in reducing risks and penalty.

Which judge within the United States is in charge of melting these sanctions or making investors pay should they fall behind in the personal or governmental investments in rental property

The United States, matters related to property disputes or sanctions as well as legal action are generally addressed by a variety of courts at various levels of authority. The particular court in question will be determined by the type and the scope of the matter. These are the court cases that could arise:

Small Claims Court: For small disputes that involve property rentals, for instance disagreements over security deposits, or damages of a minor amount, the parties are often able to seek resolution by submitting small claims to courts. Small claims courts are created to simplify and speedy process that allows the parties to be represented by themselves and with no lawyer.

State Civil Courts To resolve major disputes regarding rental property including eviction actions or breach of lease agreements and larger claims for financial damages The cases could be filed within the civil courts of the specific state. Every State has its own courts and the particular court that is part of the system is based on the court's jurisdictional rules as well as the monetary limits for each court.

Federal Courts: in a few situations, the dispute over rent property can involve federal laws or constitutional questions including unfair housing laws or claims for discrimination.

They can be taken to the federal district court in the event that they fall within the federal court's the jurisdiction of federal courts.

It's crucial to know that the courts and their procedures may be different between state and local authorities. It's recommended to speak with an attorney who is specialized in the field of real estate law or landlord-tenant law, to learn about the specific procedures and rules of jurisdiction that apply to your particular circumstances.

Chapter 7: Rental Properties Investment

Rental property investment is an extremely popular kind of real estate investment in which individuals or firms acquire properties with the aim to generate rent. This involves purchasing commercial or residential properties, as well as renting them to tenants that pay rent on a monthly basis in exchange for use of the house.

The idea of investing in rental properties could be a lucrative investment because of a number of factors. First, it offers an ongoing source of passive income from rental income, which could be used to fund the cost of mortgages, costs as well as generate potential profits. In addition, rental properties possess the possibility of gaining value over time that allows investors to gain by the increase in value of their property in the course of time.

In the case of considering investment in rental properties It is crucial to consider a variety of factors. It is crucial to consider the location since properties located in locations with quality infrastructure, amenities, as well as close proximity to schools, transportation and commercial areas are likely to draw tenants as well as generate higher rents. Furthermore, aspects such as conditions of the property, market demand as well as rental rates and the local laws should be taken into consideration.

There are many kinds of rental properties comprising residential ones (such as single-family houses, condos, apartments) and commercial property (such as office buildings and retail space, as well as industrial property). Each has their particular advantages and disadvantages, and investors must decide based upon their goals for investing along with their financial capability as well as market analysis.

The ability of investors to finance investment in rental properties using a variety of options, like conventional mortgages, cash purchase or partnership. It is crucial to evaluate the financial viability of your investment by taking into account things like the amount of the down payment, regular costs (property taxes and insurance costs, maintenance) and the possibility of vacancies in addition to cash flow estimates.

The management of rental properties includes duties like the screening and finding of tenants and collecting rent, managing maintaining the property, and dealing with tenant issues or concerns. Investors have the option of managing the property themselves, or contract firms to manage the responsibilities, for a cost.

Investment in rental properties can yield lucrative returns as well as diversification of the portfolio of investments. It is important to do exhaustive research, conduct due diligence, and obtain an expert's advice before taking any investment choices on the market for real estate.

Chapter 8: Benefits Of Rental Properties Investing

Renting properties can provide many benefits to those who invest. These are the top benefits:

1. Continuous Cash Flow property is a steady and steady source of income from rent payments. The steady flow of cash can be used to pay mortgages as well as property costs, and also generate income. In contrast to other investments which depend on fluctuations in the market the rental income may provide security and stability.

2. Building equity and appreciation Property that is rented has the potential of growing in value as time passes. In the past, real estate tends to appreciate over the long time, which allows investors to gain from the property's growth. Furthermore, when the mortgage balance is paid an investor accumulates an equity stake in the home that can then be used to fund future investment or to fund a loan.

3. Tax Benefits: Property rental properties offer tax benefits of various kinds. The investor can deduct costs including property taxes insurance, mortgage interest maintenance, repairs and more which reduce their tax-deductible income. The depreciation benefit is also significant that lets investors take a percentage of the worth of their property each year and thereby lowering the burden of tax.

4. Renting properties could give diversification to an investment portfolio. It has been shown historically that real estate has an absence of correlation to other asset classes like bonds and stocks which means that its value usually is not dependent on the overall market. The addition of rental properties to your investment portfolio may aid in spreading risk and enhance the overall performance of your portfolio.

5. Control and Appreciation: As opposed to the other types of investments property, rental properties give owners a certain

amount of control. Investors have the ability to make strategic choices concerning property management, repairs rent rates, choice of tenants that can directly affect the performance of the property. Investors can also modify the property in order to increase the value of the property and boost the rental revenue.

6. Renting homes can act as an efficient hedge against the rise in inflation. Since the price of living rises rents tend to climb, and landlords can modify rents in line with the increase. This could help safeguard the buying power of your investment as well as guarantee a stable income stream that can keep pace with the rate of inflation.

7. Long-Term Asset Creation Renting properties offer the potential to be a source of creating wealth in the long term. In time, as the property increases in value as mortgage balances shrink while rental rates grow the equity of the owner as well as cash flow could dramatically improve. Properties that are

rented can be an avenue to increase wealth as well as create an income stream that can be used in the future.

8. Leverage: Investments in real estate which include rental properties allow you to utilize leverage. If you can get a loan to help finance the purchase the investor can manage the more substantial asset while making an investment that is smaller. This can increase the possible return from investments. If the property gains value, then the equity of the investor increases even though the first investment was much less.

9. A hedge against market volatility: Rental properties may act as an insurance against the volatility of markets. Although other types of investments like stocks may experience large price changes but rental properties tend to be more stable. The market for real estate generally has more steady price fluctuations which allows the investors to ride the market's volatility and keep an income stream that is steady.

10. Rent properties can be a good source of diversification for portfolios. They provide diversification advantages through the addition of an option to the portfolio of investments. The ability to diversify across various asset classes like bonds, stocks as well as real estate, will increase risk spread and decrease the volatility overall that the portfolio experiences. Properties that are rental have the capacity to offer a unique risk-return ratio compared to conventional financial instruments, thereby enhancing the diversification of your portfolio.

11. Possibility of appreciation through renovations Potential for Appreciation through Renovations: A benefit of rental properties is that they can boost their value with upgrades and renovations. When renovating the property, landlords are able to increase its appeal to attract better-quality tenants and possibly increase rent. The renovations could also cause capital appreciation because the market value could

increase due to improvements in condition and amenities.

12. Control of Investments Rent properties supply investors with an asset they are able to actively control. Contrary to other investments like stocks and mutual funds where the investor is in influence over the actual property, rental properties give investors more control. Investors have the ability to make intelligent choices regarding the management of their property as well as tenant selection and improvements to the property in order to maximize the performance of their investment.

Chapter 9: Types Of Rental Properties

There are many types of rental properties investors could consider depending on their goals for investment, budget and market conditions in the local area. Below are the most commonly used types of rental property:

A. Single-Family Homes:

They are houses that have been designed for single families or a family. These homes are extremely popular with investors because of their broad popularity and the potential to generate rent for the long term. They are popular with families or people who are looking for greater privacy and space.

Single-family houses are a sought-after and profitable option for rental investors in property. The properties are versatile and offer many advantages that make these properties a desirable investment choice.

In the first place, homes with a single family have a tendency to draw a wider selection of tenants from families to young professionals and provide a wider potential tenants. The wide market appeal boosts the chances of finding reliable as well as long-term renters.

In addition, single-family homes provide an air of seclusion and space which is sought-after by a lot of people who rent. They have their own backyard or driveway and usually several bathrooms and bedrooms, they cater to the requirements of families and people who are looking for a spacious and private living space.

In terms of investment from an investment perspective, single-family homes usually come with lower initial costs and costs for maintenance compared to multi-unit houses. Finance options are usually simpler to obtain, and the management of property is typically easier, particularly those who manage their own rental properties.

Single-family houses can reap the possibility of property appreciation as time passes. When the property market fluctuates, these homes possess the possibility of increasing in value. This will allow owners to earn equity, and possibly earn substantial gains when selling the property at some point in the future.

Single-family homes offer investors the ability to modify their investment strategies. Homeowners may choose to let the house in its entirety or look into alternatives to renting out the property, like holiday rentals or short-term rentals according to local regulations and demand.

Single-family houses offer a variety of benefits to rental property investors. These include a wide rental pool of tenants as well as privacy and security for tenants, less upfront charges and costs for maintaining as well as potential appreciation of the property as well as flexibility with the rental strategy. No matter if you're an experienced property investor or are just beginning with single-family properties, they can be the ideal choice for you to expand your portfolio of rental properties and meet your financial targets.

B. Multi-Family Properties:

Multi-family properties are made up of structures that have multiple dwelling units, like duplexes, triplexes and apartments. The investment in multi-family homes allows investors to earn numerous streams of rental revenue by dividing the units of the same building. It is a cost-effective method to expand the rental company as well as diversify income sources.

Multi-family properties, with many units in one place have a multitude of benefits that make them an ideal option for investors who are smart.

In the first place, multi-family homes offer the opportunity for diversification. By having multiple rental units within the same property, you are able to spread the risk among different sources of income. Even when one unit is unoccupied or undergoing some sort of temporary recession, others can still generate earnings, providing the stability of your cash flow.

Multi-family properties provide advantages of scale. The benefits of shared charges like maintenance, insurance, as well as utilities. This can be cheaper than managing single-family homes. This will allow you to be more efficient in the management of your portfolio of investments.

In addition, multi-family properties tend to attract tenants who are long-term. Individuals and families seeking low-cost accommodation appreciate the comfort as well as the community-oriented environment offered by multi-family homes. This can lead to less vacancy and lower turnover. This can result in a steady rental revenue.

In terms of financing from a financial standpoint, multi-family houses can provide better loan terms. Some lenders view multi-unit houses as safer due to multiple income streams which makes it simpler to obtain loans and possibly get better rate of interest.

Another attractive aspect of homes with multiple families is the chance for increased appreciation through forced effort. Through enhancing and optimizing your property with renovations, improvements to amenities or a more efficient management system it is possible to increase its value as well as generate more rental revenue, ultimately increasing the ROI on your the investment.

Multi-family houses offer a great chance to manage your property on site. The proximity of your tenants can provide better control and communication, leading to a higher level of satisfaction for tenants as well as retention.

Multi-family properties offer a thrilling and profitable option for investors in rental properties. Through built-in diversification, economics of scale, long-term tenants interest, favorable financing choices as well as the possibility of forced appreciation and even potential for management on site Multi-family houses are the potential to be a potent investment tool that will increase your wealth. Make sure you are ready to increase your investment portfolio, increase your earning potential and reap the benefits from multi-family homes.

C. Vacation Rentals:

Vacation rental properties are homes that are which are available for rental on a limited-time basis. They are usually used for vacations or short-term durations. They may include homes and apartments as well as private rooms. These properties are typically found in tourist locations or tourist spots. They can earn higher rentals during peak times however, they might also need additional management and marketing strategies.

The term "vacation rentals," also referred to as short-term rental, have seen a huge rise in popularity over recent times, and for the right reasons.

One of the most notable advantages of renting out vacation homes can be their large rental earnings. Through leveraging the boom in tourism and travel industry it is possible to draw vacationers as well as business travellers looking for exclusive and luxurious lodging. By charging higher rates, especially during the peak season and at popular destinations Vacation rentals could produce a significant flow of cash which is higher than traditional rental properties.

Rentals for vacation homes offer flexibility and the ability to control your investment. As opposed to rentals for long periods which are not flexible, vacation rentals allow you to make use of the property on private vacations at any time you want. You can take advantage of the house and still enjoy the benefits of the financial investment when you're not in use. This is like being able to enjoy cake, and have it as well!

The rental of vacation properties also offers an opportunity to make a strategic option. Making investments in tourist hot spots such as beachfront homes, lively city centers could attract an ever-growing number of visitors and increase the occupancy rate. By conducting thorough market research and knowing the needs of travellers and preferences, you are able to make educated choices to maximize your return on investment.

In addition, vacation rentals typically need less commitment than conventional investment in real estate. The best way to try it is beginning with a single property before gradually increasing your portfolio according to your experiences and your success. Additionally, due to the growth of websites for vacation rentals handling bookings, payment and communication with guests is now streamlined and easy.

Important to keep in mind that rental properties require careful control, which includes regular maintenance, cleaning as well as communication with guests. But, with the aid of property management companies, or websites for vacation rentals You can outsource a number of these tasks. This will allow you to concentrate on the financial aspect of the investment.

Rentals for vacations are a fun and lucrative investment opportunity with a high rental income potential, versatility in the use of property, strategically placed choices, and capacity. In addition, by tapping into the expanding market for travel, you will be able to benefit from the need for distinctive accommodations and make an income-producing investment portfolio. Get ready to dive into the realm of vacation rentals and start the journey of amazing experiences, financial gain and memorable memories.

There are many kinds

1. Condominiums: Condominiums or condos are parts of a larger structure or complex, which are managed in a separate manner and usually managed by a homeowners ' association (HOA). Investors may purchase condos and let them to tenants. The majority of condos offer amenities, including swimming pools fitness facilities, and common spaces, which could attract tenants who want a easy and hassle-free living.

2. Townhouses: Townhouses are generally multi-level residences that share at least two walls neighbouring properties. They are a good compromise between condominiums and homes with regard to dimensions, amenities, as well as their maintenance requirements. Townhouses may appeal to those who want larger space and more privacy in comparison to condominiums and apartments however they are priced at a lower when compared with detached homes.

3. Commercial Rental properties can include office space as well as retail and warehouses, industrial buildings. Commercial properties could bring higher yields on rental than residential properties. They will however need more capital, specialist expertise, and more lengthy lease contracts. Commercial property is often desired by companies as well as professionals and other organizations searching for the right space for their business operations.

It is crucial for investors to examine the rental demand, rates, vacancy rates as well as local laws that are specific to the type of property prior to making any investment decision. Every type of rental property has specific considerations and investors must select the one that best fits their goals and investment strategies.

4. Student Housing: These housing units are created and intended for students attending college or universities. They are situated near to schools and provide housing units for the needs of students, like sharing bedrooms, or apartments-style living. Students' housing could provide an income stream that is stable because there is a constant demand for accommodation for students in close proximity to universities and colleges.

5. Senior Living Communities These communities, sometimes referred to retirement communities, or active adult communities, are specifically designed for those who have reached the age of 65 and

are looking for independence or assisted living choices. The majority of these communities offer amenities that are specifically designed for seniors including social gatherings such as health facilities, social activities, as well as transportation. The decision to invest in senior living communities could tap into the expanding population of older people, as well as provide a steady and sustainable rental income.

6. Mixed-Use Properties: These properties are those that combine commercial and residential areas within the same building. They could be an assortment of retail areas offices, office buildings, or housing units. Investment in mixed-use properties allow the diversification of sources of income and the possibility of synergies with commercial and residential tenants. It is an appealing choice in highly-demanded or urban locations where the residents appreciate the ease of working and living at the same time.

Each kind of rental property is accompanied by particular aspects, considerations and challenges. Investors must thoroughly study and analyze the elements that pertain to the property before taking the investment decision. In addition local market conditions as well as laws must be considered for compliance, and to maximize profits from investments.

Chapter 10: Finding The Right Rental Property

The right rental property for your investment takes careful research in analysis, evaluation, and research. These are the steps you can take to assist you in finding appropriate rental properties

1. Determine your investment criteria Begin by clearly delineating your objectives for investment, budget, preferred location and property type, anticipated rent income and the the market you want to target for tenants. With clear guidelines, you to narrow your search for houses that meet your goals for investing and will limit the search.

2. Find out about the local Real Estate Market Complete a thorough study regarding the market for real estate in the area in which you plan to make investments. Examine developments in prices for properties as well as rental rates, vacant rates and general dynamic of the market. Consider factors such as the growth of population, employment

opportunities as well as infrastructure developments and facilities that could affect the need for rental property within the vicinity.

3. Make use of online listing Platforms or Real Estate Brokers Explore websites for listings, online platforms, and websites for real estate and connect with expert real estate agents that are experts in renting property. These sites can give you access to numerous property listings and give insight on the market in your area. Realtors can assist in property shows or negotiations and can provide advice based on their experience.

4. Conduct a Financial Analysis: When you've identified properties that could be yours you want to purchase, do a comprehensive review of their finances to evaluate the potential for investment. Consider factors such as the cost of purchase, rental income possible, operating expenses (including the cost of property tax and insurance and maintenance expenses) as well as financing options and the

projected cash flow. Take into consideration metrics such as caps, cash-on-cash returns and returns on investments (ROI) to evaluate various properties, and to determine the profitability of each property.

5. Examine Property Condition: Determine the condition of the house by carrying out extensive examinations. Examine for structural problems and maintenance requirements, as well as possible renovation needs. Be aware of the costs associated with repair or upgrade and include these into your budget. A house that is well-maintained could require less expenditure and could attract better-quality tenants.

6. Take into consideration the Tenant Demand and Rental Profile: Examine the rent demand within the vicinity and pinpoint the prospective tenant market that is suitable of the house. Take into consideration factors like accessibility to schools, transportation and employment facilities, as well as facilities, and preferences for lifestyle. Knowing the profile

of the tenant will assist in maintaining a consistent rent and reduce vacancies.

7. Examine Rental Market Regulations: Familiarize your self with the local regulations for rental markets like the rights of tenants rental control laws, the zoning regulations, as well as the requirements for licensing. It is vital for avoiding legal issues and guarantee a seamless rent-to-let process.

8. Conduct Due Diligence: Prior to buying a property, do extensive due diligence of the property. Check the documents related to the property, which include lease agreements, title deeds financial documents, the legal concerns. You may want to consider hiring professionals like appraisers, property inspectors as well as real estate lawyers, for assistance with the due diligence procedure.

Be aware that investing in rentals is a long-term investment, which is why it's crucial to do your study and evaluation. Consider the possibility of evaluating several properties, get expert assistance, and then make educated choices based on the criteria you choose to invest in as well as market conditions.

A. Location Location Location!! In the search for the best rental property for investment, location is an important part. The place of the rental property will significantly affect its appeal and rental demand, as well as rent quality and yields. Below are some important factors to take into consideration when looking at the property's location:

1. Economic Factors: Search for regions with a robust and varied economic. Take into consideration factors like job expansion, unemployment rate as well as major industries and whether there are established firms or new developments. A strong economy could contribute to the stability of rental markets as well as attract renters looking for job possibilities.

2. Rent Market Demand Study the rental market demand within the area you are looking at. Find areas that have an extremely

low rate of vacancy and a stable rental market. Take into consideration factors like the growth of population, patterns of migration as well as the student population (if relevant) and overall market dynamics of supply and demand within the market for rental. Locations with high demand but low supply usually have higher rentals with a higher potential for income.

3. Infrastructure and amenities: Evaluate the accessibility and quality of infrastructure and amenities in the region. Be sure to consider the proximity of schools, universities hospital, shopping malls and parks, as well as public transportation and many other facilities. The majority of tenants prefer renting houses in areas that offer ease of access to the essential services as well as recreational amenities.

4. Safety in the neighborhood: Security is a major issue for renters. Find out the rates of crime as well as the safety of your neighborhood and the quality of the community. Look for areas with the lowest

crime rate and have an image of being secure and welcoming to families. Homes in areas with safer communities tend to draw more desirable tenants, and may command more rent.

5. Districts for Schools: When looking to attract tenants from families, you should consider the reputation of the district's local schools. Property located in areas that have well-known schools are often searched for by those who are seeking a high-quality education for their kids. The accessibility to schools that are of high quality can boost property value and demand for rental.

6. Future Development and Infrastructure Projects Consider any proposed or ongoing infrastructure project, for example, new hubs for transportation commercial projects, public facilities. They can increase areas' appeal and increase the value of property and draw many more potential tenants. But be aware of possible disruptions that could occur during stages of construction.

7. Local regulations: Get familiar with the local laws such as zoning laws and the rental market's policies that are specific for the area. There are some areas that have restrictions regarding short-term rentals and rent control rules and licensing rules which can affect the profit and the viability of investing.

8. Potential for Long-Term Appreciation: Take into consideration the possibility of appreciation in the future for the area. Market trends and historical data will provide insight into real estate value growth in the region as time passes. Regions that experience expansion, urban renewal, or improvement to infrastructure usually have an opportunity for appreciation over the long term.

Additional points to consider

1. Lease Laws and Regulations Be familiar with lease laws and regulations that apply to your location. Know your rights as a tenant and eviction procedures, security deposit rules, and the other laws that could impact

the rental company. It is vital in order to prevent legal problems and to ensure smooth operations.

2. Property Taxes: Find out the rates of property taxes for the area. The higher property tax rates can chip the rental revenue and reduce your overall profits. Examine the tax rates for property taxes in various areas in order to determine the right balance between desired location and tax burdens that are manageable.

3. The market supply and competition Examine the current availability of rental homes at the site. In a market that is over-saturated, it could cause higher vacancies, and, in turn, lower rental prices. But an area with low availability and a large demand may provide better rental income. Be aware of competition from other landlords as well as the equilibrium between demand and supply in the region.

4. Transportation and accessibility: Consider the ease of access to the area. Be sure to

consider the location's proximity to major highways, public transport alternatives, airports and other hubs for transportation. Locations that are close to public transportation may be more appealing to potential tenants, and could attract more tenants.

5. Local Lifestyle and Community The overall aspects of the community as well as the lifestyles that are present in the area. Search for neighborhoods that offer an underlying spirit of community, as well as leisure facilities, cultural offerings as well as entertainment choices. The properties in desirable and vibrant areas often draw tenants looking for an excellent quality of life.

6. Climate and Natural Disasters: Take into consideration the climate and dangers of natural disasters within the vicinity. Certain areas are susceptible to earthquakes, hurricanes, wildfires or floods. Examine the insurance requirements as well as the risks that could be related to the particular

location. Property owners in areas that have a high risk of natural catastrophes might require additional insurance as well as contingency plans.

7. Planning for Long-Term Development: Study the development plans that are long-term or urban renewal projects within the area. The areas that undergo revitalization and infrastructure upgrades could offer opportunities to increase the value of property as well as rental demand. Be aware of changes that might influence the attractiveness and potential growth of the area.

It's essential to fully study and evaluate the area prior to investing in rental property. Being aware of the local market's dynamic as well as rental demand and tenants' preferences can help you make educated decisions, and increase potential return on the investment.

B. Property Condition

Assessing the condition of rental properties is a crucial aspect in selecting the ideal investment. The condition of the property can affect the potential for rental income and ongoing maintenance expenses, and even the level of satisfaction among tenants. These are the most important considerations to consider when looking at the condition of a rental property

1. Structural Integrity: Examine the structure of your property, which includes the walls, foundation as well as the roof and floors. Examine for indications of structural problems like cracks, sagging or water damages. An enduring and well-maintained structure is crucial to the sustainability of a home.

2. plumbing and Electrical Systems: Examine the electrical and plumbing system that are in the building. Examine the condition of plumbing and fixtures, as well as the pressure in the water and leaks. Check the electrical wiring outlets, as well as the operation of circuit breakers and switches. Renovating or

replacing such systems is costly and therefore, make sure they're functioning properly.

3. HVAC Systems: Check the HVAC, heating, as well as cooling (HVAC) HVAC systems. Verify the age, condition and function of the air conditioner, furnace as well as ventilation systems. A properly functioning HVAC system is essential for the comfort of tenants and could affect energy efficiency as well as the cost of maintenance.

4. Interior Condition: Assess the interior of the home, including ceilings, walls as well as flooring and fixtures. Check for evidence of wear and wear, water damage, insects, or mold. Think about the aesthetic appeal of the home and decide if any cosmetic improvements or repairs are needed.

5. External Condition: Check the exterior of the building such as the roof, siding windows as well as the landscaping. Check for evidence of deterioration or damage or repairs that are required. Maintaining your exterior will

improve appearance and increases the satisfaction of tenants.

6. appliances and amenities: Evaluate the state of appliances that are part of the property rental including refrigerators, stoves, dishwashers and washing appliances. Examine their condition, age and the possibility of repair or replacement. Think about any other amenities like a swimming fitness center or pool, as well as the condition of their equipment and maintenance needs.

7. Maintenance History: Ask regarding the maintenance history of the property as well as any repair or remodels. Examine any documents or receipts issued for previous maintenance tasks. The knowledge of the property's needs for maintenance and past can give insight about its general condition as well as possible future expenses.

8. Conformity to Building Codes and Safety Standards Check that your property is in compliance with the local codes for building and safety requirements. Verify for

outstanding infractions or permits required. The compliance with rules is crucial in order to ensure the security of tenants as well as avoid legal problems.

It's recommended that you hire experienced inspectors or contractors who can thoroughly evaluate the property's condition. They are able to spot any problems or risks which may not be obvious in a physical assessment. The condition of the house can help estimate repairs or remodeling costs, incorporate these into your analysis of financials to make an educated choice about whether the investment is viable.

Further points to consider

1. Maintenance Requirements: Examine the maintenance needs for the building. Take note of the condition and age of key components including the roofing and plumbing systems, as well as electrical and HVAC. Consider if urgent or continuing repairs or maintenance are required. Property with less maintenance needs might result in fewer

interruptions as well as costs over the renting duration.

2. Energy Efficiency: Examine your energy efficiency and the building. Find features such as insulation, windows that are energy efficient, as well as updated appliances to aid in reducing utility bills. The energy-efficient homes can draw environmentally aware tenants and may result in lower operating costs.

3. Safety features: Think about the existence of security features within the building for example, carbon monoxide detectors, extinguishers for fire and security systems for entry. Making sure that the living space is safe for tenants is vital and could help minimize the risk of liability.

4. Storage and Parking: Evaluate the condition and availability of storage facilities as well as parking space. Find out if there's enough parking space for tenants and if storage facilities, like garages or basements are readily available. These facilities could add

value to the property, and draw tenants who have special needs.

5. Accessibility and universal Design Consider the property's accessibility facilities, specifically in the event that you are planning to reach tenants from a variety of backgrounds. Think about features like ramps, wide doorways and bathrooms with accessible toilets that can accommodate those with disabilities in mobility. Design features that are universal can increase the appeal of your property to a larger selection of potential tenants.

6. Conformity to Local Housing Standards: Ensure that the building meets local regulations and standards regarding housing. Verify that the property is in compliance with the building code as well as health and safety rules and other specific rules applicable to rental properties in the region. Failure to comply could result in penalties and legal problems, as well as issues in attracting and retaining tenants.

7. Durability and longevity: Take into consideration the longevity and durability of the material and finish that are used to construct the home. Choose materials that need minimal maintenance or replacement. The durability of the features will help reduce cost of repairs, and also contribute to long-term viability of your purchase.

8. Concerns about mold and pests Check for evidence of pest issues, including pests or insects, in addition to issues with mildew and mold. The effects of these issues could be harmful to the health of the building or health of the tenants, as well as its image. The resolution of mold or pest issues immediately is vital to keep the health and comfort of your living space.

When you thoroughly evaluate the state of a property, you are able to anticipate possible expenses, determine the potential of your investment as well as make educated decisions. A well-maintained property is likely to attract top tenants, lower turnover and reduce unplanned maintenance expenses, leading to a profitable rental investment.

C. Financing

Finding the most suitable financing solution to invest in your rental property is a crucial step in the whole process. Below are the most important considerations in the financing process:

1. Establish your Budget: Begin by setting your budget to invest in a rental property. Examine your budget which include savings, investments, as well as a possible down payments. A clear understanding of your budget can aid you in determining the cost for the properties you could manage and help you make financial decision making.

2. Consider Mortgage Options: Explore the various mortgage options that are available for financing your rental property. Conventional mortgages, loans backed by the government (such such as FHA as well as VA loans) and portfolio loans are popular

options. Compare rates, conditions and conditions for down payments, and eligibility criteria for every kind of loan. Contact mortgage lenders to know the requirements for each type of loan and the rates that are available to you.

3. Look into Financing Strategies: Consider the various ways to finance your business and increase the returns on your investments. You could, for instance, think about a leveraged investment, for example using a mortgage that has a lower down payment as well as taking on a bigger percentage of the home's cost of purchase. This can allow the possibility of boosting the returns of your investment if properties rise as time passes.

4. Loan Pre-Approval: Prior to seeking properties, you should consider applying for pre-approval to a mortgage. The pre-approval proves your reliability as a potential buyer, and can help to streamline the buying process. This gives you an accurate picture of your loan capacity and permits you to submit

an offer that is competitive when you locate an appropriate property.

5. Assess the cost of financing Alongside an interest charge, take into consideration the financing expenses that are that are associated with the loan. Consider things like closing costs along with origination fees, point and various other costs. Examine different loan options to determine the most affordable choice for your financial needs.

6. Cash Flow Analysis: Conduct an analysis of the flow of cash to determine if the property can generate positive cash flow, after taking into account financing costs. Think about the possibility of rental income and operating expenses, as well as insurance, property taxes as well as mortgage payment. A positive cash flow is essential to ensure the sustainability of your investment and give you a profit on capital.

7. Investment Property Loans If you are planning to purchase several rental properties, you should look into the various

investment property loan options. These loans are specifically designed to be used by real estate investors, and could have unique conditions and requirements as compared to traditional mortgages. These loans are typically characterized by greater requirements for the down payment and can have you meet specific requirements pertaining to your real property portfolio.

8. Other financing options: Take a look at alternatives to financing, like crowdfunding platforms, private lenders or partnership with investors from other sources. These alternatives can give you the flexibility to access capital in situations where traditional financing might not be practical or accessible.

Further ideas

1. Check the requirements of a down payment to determine the best financing option. Conventional mortgages generally need a down payment at least 20% to invest in properties. But, there are other choices that could permit a smaller down payment,

for example the government-backed loan or some loans for investment properties. Review your funds available and figure out the minimum down payment amount that you can afford.

2. Inflation Rates Compare rate of interest from various loan and lending institutions. The impact of interest rates on your mortgage monthly payments as well as the overall return on investment. Find the most favorable rates and conditions, taking into consideration the fixed rate and adjustable rate mortgages. The lower rate of interest could help boost liquidity and improve the ROI on investments.

3. A Loan Term: Think about the length of your period of your loan as well as its effects on your investment strategies. Shorter-term loans (15 and 20 years) generally come with lower interest rates, however higher monthly installments. Loan terms that are longer like 30 years could result in less monthly installments, but could lead to higher interest

rates in the long run. The loan's term should be aligned to your goals for investment and cash flow forecasts.

4. Creditworthiness: Check your creditworthiness and score prior to applying for credit. A higher score on your credit generally will result in lower rate of interest and terms for loans. Review your credit reports to identify any errors or issues which require your care. Make steps to boost your credit score by making sure you pay your bills punctually, cutting down on credit card debt and ensuring an excellent score on your credit utilization.

5. Reserves for Cash: Lenders might need to see cash reserves prior to approving the loan to invest in a property. Cash reserves serve as a protection to pay for unexpected costs or to cover times of vacant. Examine your financial position and be sure to have sufficient reserves as well as cash reserves for down payments and closing expenses.

6. The Loan-to-Value Ratio: Know the value-for-loan (LTV) ratio. It represents the proportion of the property's value the lender will fund. Most lenders will have LTV limitations in the case of investments. An lower LTV ratio could result in better loan terms. Find the LTV ratio lenders like and then plan your financial plan according to that.

7. Tax implications: Take a look at the tax implications when investing in rental properties. The interest on mortgages, property taxes as well as certain costs could be tax deductible and reduce the overall tax burden. Talk to a tax expert to learn more about the tax benefits as well as the consequences to the purchase.

Chapter 11: Managing Your Rental Properties

The management of your rental properties efficiently is essential to maximize your profits and making sure that tenants are satisfied. Three essential aspects to consider when managing rental properties effectively:

A. Tenant Screening

Tenant screening and selection: Set up a comprehensive tenant screening procedure to identify trustworthy and accountable tenants. The screening process can include background checks, confirming earnings and employment, looking up the rental history, as well as obtaining references. Selecting tenants that meet the requirements and are reputable will reduce the chance of late payment as well as property damage. the possibility of eviction.

Tenant screening is an essential procedure that allows you to identify trustworthy and responsible tenants to the rental home you own. If you conduct thorough tenant screening it will lower your risk of having issues such as late payment damages to property, late payments, or expulsion. These are some of the most important guidelines for conducting effective screening of tenants:

1. Application Process: Implement an application procedure that is standard for prospective tenants. Fill out a rental form which collects the essential details like personal information such as earnings history, employment history as well as rental history and references. Be sure to fill in their application completely and then sign the form.

2. The Credit Report: Request consent from applicants to run a credit inquiry. This lets you assess their financial responsibilities and record of paying their due bills and debts punctually. Get credit reports from reliable credit bureaus and examine them for any indicators of negatives including late payments and collection accounts or excessive debt.

3. Verification of Income and Employment Validate the applicant's earnings and employment by asking for pay stubs, letters from employment or tax returns. This will ensure that they earn a consistent income that can pay their debts. Take into consideration a minimum requirement for income and assess the income of the applicant relative to the rent.

4. Verification of Rental History: Call former landlords to confirm the tenant's history of renting. Find out about their history of payments as well as their adherence to lease agreements as well as any other issues or issues during their tenure. Find out about the notice period and whether they have left their prior rental in a good state. An excellent rental record can indicate the responsibleness of a tenant.

5. Background Check: Perform background checks to determine the criminal record of applicants. This will ensure the security and security of tenants as well as the building it

self. Examine any convictions for criminality that are related to drug or violence or damage to property. Follow fair housing law and regulations when evaluating background checks for criminal convictions.

6. Contact References: Make contact with personal references supplied by candidates to get further insight on their character, trustworthiness and ability to be tenants. References are a great source of data about the applicants' behavior or lifestyle as well as ability to create a pleasant living space.

7. Fair Housing Compliance Respect the fair housing rules and regulations to ensure your tenant screening procedure is impartial and fair. Do not discriminate that is based on gender, race, religion or disability situation. Create clear and consistent guidelines to determine the tenant's selection criteria that are applied uniformly for each applicant.

8. Be aware of your instincts during the process of screening take note of your instincts and feelings concerning the

prospective tenant. If you notice something that is off or causes you to be concerned It's crucial to consider your feelings. Although it is important to be able to rely on the facts however, your intuition can give you valuable information.

Always seek the written permission of applicants for background checks, credit check, as well as verification of rent and employment histories. Make your screening guidelines clear with applicants prior to the interview and use the same procedure in order to ensure an equal treatment. Keep a record of all decisions and interactions that were made during the screening procedure in case you need to reference them later.

Tenant screening is a crucial method of identifying reliable and trustworthy tenants who are able to maintain the property as well as pay rent on time and adhere to the provisions of the lease. Through thorough screenings, you will be able to reduce risks and provide a pleasant rent experience for both the tenants and you.

B. Maintenance and repairs Property Maintenance and Repairs Maintain and inspect regularly your properties for rental to ensure that you maintain them in good shape. Repairs and maintenance issues should be addressed promptly in order to maintain tenant satisfaction and stop small issues that could become costly issues. Build relationships with trusted contractor and services in order to take care of repairs quickly.

Maintaining and repairing are vital elements of managing the rental property. Effectively dealing with maintenance issues and completing timely repairs not just ensures satisfaction of tenants as well as protects your investment. Below are some important tips in managing repair and maintenance:

1. Periodic Property Inspections Make periodic inspections of the rental property in order to determine any repairs or

maintenance needs. Inspections help to spot tiny issues before they develop into serious issues and be a good way to ensure tenants have adhered to the provisions of your lease contract. Make sure to schedule inspections in the right timeframes taking into consideration factors like the size of your property, how many tenants are in and the condition of the property.

2. Rapid Response: Require tenants to bring up maintenance concerns promptly. Create clear channels that allow tenants to contact either you or your property management team. React to maintenance requests promptly and address concerns of tenants. Quick responses show tenants that their wellbeing is an important concern and prevents the possibility of further harm or disruption.

3. Determine Maintenance Priorities: Examine the maintenance needs based on the urgency of their request and possible consequences for tenant safety as well as property health.

The priority should be given to repairs that impact security or habitability as well as important services (e.g. heating, plumbing or electricity). Create a method for categorizing maintenance requests, and define time frames for responding based on the seriousness of the problem.

4. Trustworthy Contractors and Vendors Develop relationships with dependable vendors and contractors who are able to quickly and effectively handle the tasks of maintenance and repairs. Get recommendations from friends, get numerous quotes and check the insurance and qualifications of the vendors you collaborate with. Having a reliable network of experts can speed up repairs and guarantees high-quality work.

5. Preventative Maintenance: Establish an preventative maintenance plan to deal with potential problems before they occur. Check and maintain regularly important components in your home like plumbing systems, HVAC

systems electrical and the structural components. Do routine maintenance like cleaning the of gutters, replacing filters as well as ensuring that there are no leaks. If you address minor maintenance issues in advance, you'll be able to prevent major problems later on in the future.

6. Maintain and document maintenance Document and track maintenance. Keep a detailed record of all maintenance request repair requests, as well as the associated cost. Record the date that the service request is made. Also, document as well as the issue addressed, the steps performed, as well as the costs you incur. This document serves as a history record that helps in tracking expenditures as well as proving your promptness in responding and the compliance of maintenance requirements.

7. Plan for maintenance budget: Place the portion of your rental earnings for repairs and maintenance. Making a budget will ensure that you can cover emergencies or regular

maintenance chores. Be aware of the condition and age of your home when you decide the amount to be allocated for the maintenance costs. If your property is well maintained, it's less likely to face major issues, and it can also help to draw and keep top tenants.

8. Communication with Tenants: Make sure to keep tenants up-to-date on repair and maintenance tasks. Update them on the progress of their request, inform them about the scheduled maintenance schedule as well as provide guidelines for tenants to follow when making repairs. Communication that is clear and prompt helps maintain expectations for tenants and builds the development of a healthy connection.

9. Conformity with Local Laws: Familiarize yourself with local regulations and laws regarding the maintenance of your property and repair. Be aware of your responsibilities as a landlord, which includes obligations to deal with concerns regarding health and

safety and creating a living space that is habitable. Be sure to comply with all legal requirements for example, like completing the necessary checks or obtaining permits to make certain renovations.

10. Take a look at maintenance contracts in certain situations there may be a need to establish maintenance agreements with companies that provide services. If, for instance, you manage multiple properties, signing a contract with a trustworthy HVAC professional or landscaping business can give regular service at a lower price. Maintenance agreements can simplify procedures and guarantee that you maintain the condition of particular parts of your home.

11. Lease agreements: Write complete and clear lease agreements which outline the rights and obligations for both landlords and tenants. Include crucial details like rental amount as well as due dates and lease length, as well as guidelines and rules regarding maintenance, as well as methods for dealing

with repair and dispute. Make sure that the tenants read and comprehend the lease prior to signing it.

C. Rent collection

Rent Collection: Create the proper system to facilitate promptly collecting rent. It is important to clearly communicate the methods of payment for rent such as due dates, payment deadlines, and penalties for late payment. Think about offering payment options that are convenient like online payment for timely rent payment. Be sure to follow up with any non-payments and adhere to the terms of your lease contract.

Rent collection is a crucial component in managing rentals. This ensures you get regular and reliable rental revenue and is vital to the success of your financial investment. Below are some important considerations to ensure rent collection is effective:

1. Affirmative Rent Collection Policies It is important to clearly communicate your

policies regarding rent collection to your tenants at the very beginning. Be sure to include information about the date of due and acceptable payment options as well as late fees and any penalties for late payment. It helps to establish standards and makes sure that tenants know their rights in relation to rent payments.

2. The Lease Contract must be written. You should have an agreement in writing which clearly defines the conditions of the rent payment, which include the due date, amount and payment options that are acceptable. It is important that tenants read and agree to the lease contract before they move into. The lease agreement provides legal guidelines to collect rent and acts as a source of reference in the event dispute.

3. Different Payment Options: Offer tenants with the convenience of flexible and convenient payment choices. You can accept a range of payment methods, such as checks, cash, transfer or even the online payment

platform. By offering a variety of payment options, it allows tenants to pay rent in dates.

4. Set up a regular Rent Collection Calendar: Choose the due date of rent payments, for example the 1st of the month. Don't let tenants pay rent on a on a whim, since it may result in inconsistent payment schedules and can make the process of tracking the payment process more difficult. Instruct tenants to pay rent promptly by clearly specifying when the rent is due, and by sending prompt reminders.

5. Pay online with online payment portals. Think about setting up an online system of payment which allows tenants to pay rent online. The online platforms make it easier for tenants, and speed up the process of collecting rent for landlords. The platforms typically provide features like automated reminders, periodic payments and electronic rent receipts.

6. Quick Rent Reminders: Email reminders to tenants several days in advance of the rent

due date. It serves as a soft push to ensure tenants are in the loop with their rent payment obligations. Use different channels of communication like texts, email or web-based portals in order to make sure reminders get through to tenants in a timely manner.

7. The Late Fee Policy Define the late fee policy, and add it to your lease contract. The lease agreement should specify the sum of the late fee in the event that it's applicable and what happens if you make repeated payment delays. Incentivizing late fee payments can encourage tenants to make timely payments as well as compensate for administration costs or inconveniences caused due to late payments.

8. Continuous Follow-Up In the event that a tenant is unable to pay rent by the date due, immediately monitor the tenant. Be professional and seek out what caused the delay in payments. There are times when there could be valid reasons behind the delay.

Open dialogue can resolve the issue. If needed, you can take the appropriate steps according to the lease agreement as well as the local law.

9. Document Rental Payments: Keep precise records of each rent payment received. Make copies of all checks for bank statements or electronic payment receipts. Documentation that is accurate can aid in the preparation of tax returns, accounting and in settling disputes which may be arising in the future.

10. Enforce Rent Collection Policies: Be consistent in enforcing your rent collection policies. All tenants should be treated fairly and equally. Ensure that all tenants are held accountable for their obligations to pay rent. This is a good precedent, and helps tenants prioritize rent payments.

11. Professionalism and Courtesy: Show a respectful and professional manner in dealing with tenants about rent payment. Effective communication, empathy and the ability to

listen will help in establishing trusting relations with tenants.

12. Early Rent Rewards: You might consider providing incentives to tenants who make sure they keep their rent in check or prior to the deadline. This could take it's form of modest rental reduction or even a tiny gift or incentive. The incentive program can help tenants prioritize rent payments and build an environment of trust between the tenant and you.

13. Rent Collection Automation Consider automated systems for rent collection which streamline the process and simplify administrative duties. The systems are able to automatically collect rent payment, email tenants reminders, and keep track of the history of payments. Automation reduces the chance of errors, cuts down time and assures constant rent payment collection.

14. Clear and open communication Keep open communication lines with your tenants about rent collections. Let them know to get in

touch with you in the event that they are facing issues with making rent payments. Engaging in discussions about issues could help to discover solutions that can be mutually beneficial for example, such as changing the repayment schedule or establishing an installment program.

15. Individualized Follow-Up: Adjust your approach to communication to meet the specific needs of each tenant and specific circumstances. Certain tenants might appreciate a gentle reminder just a few days prior to the date of due, while some may need more precise contact if they struggle in making timely payment. A personal approach could aid in establishing a positive connection with tenants.

16. Grace Periods: Think about implementing the grace period of a few days following the due date for rent prior to imposing late fees. The grace period gives tenants to pay their rent without incurring any additional costs.

Make clear the length of the grace time in the lease contract to prevent confusion.

17. Continuous Documentation: Create an efficient record-keeping procedure for all documents related to rent, which includes lease agreements, payment receipts, correspondence and late payment notices. Documentation that is transparent keeps a record of the past when there are disputes or legal actions.

18. The possibility of eviction is a last resort The eviction process can be a legally-enforceable remedy to stop rent payments, it must be considered as the last option. The process of eviction can be lengthy expensive, as well as lead to a property being vacant. Explore all options like bargaining, payments arrangements, or seeking mediation prior to initiating the Eviction proceedings.

19. Legal Compliance: Get familiar with local laws for landlords and tenants, as well as rules governing rent collection. Being aware of the rights and legal obligations of tenants

as well as landlords makes sure that you manage rent collection legally-sound method. Talk to legal experts to make sure you are in that you are in compliance with the laws applicable to your situation.

20. Continuous Evaluation: Continually review your processes for collecting rent in order to determine areas where you can improve. Get feedback from your tenants about their experience in paying rent and look for methods to make your process more effective and efficient. Refining and adapting your strategy in response to feedback and changes in conditions can improve rent collection processes.

www.ingramcontent.com/pod-product-compliance
Lightning Source LLC
Chambersburg PA
CBHW071222103326
41597CB00016B/1910